EUGENIO MONTALE

SELECTED POEMS

EUGENIO MONTALE

SELECTED POEMS

INTRODUCTION BY
GLAUCO CAMBON

NEW DIRECTIONS

Certain of these translations were first published in the special
Montale issue of *Quarterly Review of Literature*, copyright ©
1962, to which special acknowledgment is made. The George Kay
translations first appeared in Eugenio Montale: *Poesie/Poems*,
published by Edinburgh University Press. Some of the transla-
tions, in slightly different form, have appeared in *The Atlantic*,
Briarcliff Quarterly, *Chelsea Magazine*, *Cronos*, *Origin*, *Poetry*,
and *Voices*, to whom acknowledgment is made.

The Italian text of the Montale poems is reprinted by permission
of Arnoldo Mondadori Editore, publishers of *Ossi di Seppia*,
Le Occasione, and *La bufera e altro*. All rights reserved by
Arnoldo Mondadori Editore.

"The Eel," and "News from (Mount) Amiata" Reprinted with per-
mission of Farrar, Straus & Giroux, Inc., and Faber & Faber, Ltd.
from *Imitations* by Robert Lowell copyright © 1960 and 1961 by
Robert Lowell.

Library of Congress catalog card number: 65-15669

ISBN: 0-8112-0119-8

Manufactured in the United States of America.
New Directions books are printed on acid-free paper.

Published simultaneously in Canada by Penguin Books Canada Limited.

New Directions books are published for James Laughlin
by New Directions Publishing Corporation,
80 Eighth Avenue, New York 10011.

SIXTH PRINTING

CONTENTS

LA BUFERA E ALTRO
THE STORM AND OTHER THINGS

EUGENIO MONTALE: AN INTRODUCTION

by Glauco Cambon

Eugenio Montale, born in 1896, shares with the slightly older Giuseppe Ungaretti the honor of having led modern Italian poetry beyond the turmoil of experimentalism which had marked the opening decades of our century to an enduring achievement. This presentation of his selected verse to American readers is thus an act of belated poetic justice to one who, in a way, is a pioneer figure.

Despite his cosmopolitan circle of literary acquaintances, Montale, temperamentally no d'Annunzio, shunned campaigning for an early international reputation. But what Montale lacked in self-advertising talent and in help from combative brethren, he made up for by sheer persistence; and this is the force which appears in his poetry, to say it with the critic Contini, as a "self-built grace," though I would rather call it a relentlessness of style. Outwardly uneventful, our poet's life fits that pattern of persistence very well; it is a life without flamboyance, without carefully cultivated legends, without diffusion. It prompts us, retroactively, to think of the capital role that verbs like "to exist," "to resist," and "to endure" play in some of Montale's strongest poems, for instance "Dora Markus," where these essential attributes descried by the poet in his absent lady may be said to reverberate on his own person.

To speak of uneventfulness in a poet's life is dangerous, because his private events may be of undecipherably crucial importance, especially in the case of a man who, though far from unsociable, has kept his private life out of the limelight. Besides, the ultimately significant events of a poet's life are his poems, and to this extent Montale's existence cannot be called uneventful at all. In this connection, it will help to keep in mind how a major point of Montale's poetry has consistently been the revaluation of the personal sphere against the intrusions of loud or manufactured public reality.

Of course, public history has claimed its share of this withdrawn writer's life. Montale saw action as an infantry officer in the World War I trenches, and this experience, which was the costly education of so many writers of his generation and sometimes their physical undoing, left its mark on his writing, though less obviously than one might have expected. Unlike Giuseppe Ungaretti, Wilfred Owen, Guillaume Apollinaire, or August Stramm, Montale did not write at the time anything that could be properly called "war verse," yet the repercussion of that first holocaust of the century is to be felt in the atmosphere of hopelessness which recurrently visits his poetry; sometimes, also, sudden memories of the ordeal by fire in the rocky Tirol region gush up through the surface of a different scene in poems written decades later.

One can better appreciate Montale's (or Ungaretti's) response to war as a predicament which lays bare our essential humanity, when one compares it with the contemporary stance of Gabriele d'Annunzio, who took the same war as an inexhaustible occasion for heroic utterances. D'Annunzio's series of beaux gestes, culminating in 1918 in his flight over Vienna to shower not bombs but courteously worded invitations to surrender, commands respect in itself, but the resultant poetical harvest has in the main wilted as Montale's own verse has not.

For Montale, the war was an education to disenchantment, rather than to theatrical heroism, as his 1916 poem "Meriggiare pallido e assorto" (The Wall) may show with its sober delineation of a torrid landscape emblematic of man's fate—to follow a forbidding wall "in bewilderment." Yet it cannot be said of this well-read and largely self-educated poet that the war was his university, for that would disregard the paramount role that literary practice as such has always played in his creative career. The *métier* was his best school; and this makes him typical of an age when most of the decisive literary figures of Italy won high honors in their trade without earning university degrees.

During the war years, Montale had gravitated with other young writers to the avantgarde magazine, *La Brigata,* edited by Francesco Meriano, an enterprising litterateur who corresponded with Apollinaire. After the war, he did not join the dominant *Ronda* movement, which pleaded for a kind of classical restoration to supersede the pre-war turbulence instigated by Futurism; he founded instead, with the critics Solmi and Debenedetti, a journal of his own, *Primo Tempo* (1922), which he co-edited in Turin for the eight numbers it lasted. Though he agreed with the *Rondisti* in preferring careful chisel-work to continued yawps and fireworks, he kept a far more open mind toward the surprises of the new. Thus we find him actively supporting, or contributing to, alert magazines of the twenties like *Il Baretti,* *Il Convegno, L'Esame,* and, later, *Solaria.* These were, without exception, rallying points for the liberal intellectuals who refused to go along with the official myths of the Fascist Establishment.

The significance of such élite dissenters can hardly be exaggerated in the context of Fascist Italy. Even when they abstained from overt political opposition, they kept alive the tradition of independent thinking and artistic integrity, which is to say that they made writers like Eugenio Montale possible. It was one of the liberal editors, Piero Gobetti of Turin, who published Montale's first volume of verse, *Ossi di*

Seppia (Cuttlefish Bones), in 1925. At twenty-nine, its author was spelling the new word in Italian poetry, and without indulging in arrogant antics; the book bore the unmistakable mark of observant maturity. The poems register political despondency, though they do so by mere implication, unlike Montale's far more outspoken pieces to come with World War II. The former were written in the aftermath of World War I and under the shadow of tightening dictatorship, and they denounce this predicament by seeing through the official buoyancy to a threatening paralysis. This can best be seen in the negative statement, at once ethical and aesthetic, of a piece like "Non chiederci la parola" (Twisted of Briar), where the poet declares himself incapable of any world-disclosing utterance, for he and his likes can only define themselves by negation, by saying what they "are not," what they "do not desire." And in the far more elaborate self-portrait, "Arsenio," we see him face the "miscarried prodigies" of his own "stifled" existence.

Montale's verse is not inevitably pitched to this somber note, to which, indeed, poems like "Quasi una Fantasia" (Almost a Fantasy), "Mediterraneo" (Mediterranean), and later "L'Anguilla" (The Eel) provide an affirmative antiphon. The age evokes from him a stoic *No* for the sake of the vital values in which he believes, and that is what gives his rare affirmations such a sharp edge and relevance. One is reminded at this point that this visionary poet harbors in himself an exacting critic. As with Valéry and Eliot (whom Montale was soon to recognize as a kindred spirit), the critic has operated both inside the poetry and outside. A comprehensive edition of Montale's criticism is now (1965) still being assembled from the several journals to which he has contributed through the years. The critic is in his case what we might expect him to be: curious, undogmatic, selective, armed with a "divining rod" and not with a system. Criticism as rhabdomancy is what he advocated recently in a short note for *Il Corriere della Sera,* the leading daily to which he regularly contributes; the image is revelatory in its uncanny aptness. It equates poetry with the waters of life, and it implies that these waters may be rare and hidden under a barren soil. One thinks of the stony landscapes in Montale's first book, and of his ever renewed, if often frustrated, quest for a sign of life in the midst of that barrenness.

One also realizes that, in a sense, Montale the critic is just as decidely a poet in his openness to contingency as Montale the writer of verse; it is the divining rod of his highly educated sensitivity that made him discover Italo Svevo in 1925, a discovery amounting to a self-recognition since Svevo's muffled prose, Svevo's urbane pessimism, Svevo's irony are germane to Montale's stern vision and style. The same divining rod, we should add, afforded Montale the elusive epiphanies of "Mottetti" (Motets, a central sequence in his volume *Occasioni*).

In 1927 he moved to Florence as curator of the Vieusseux Library. He was to lose this congenial position in 1938 for refusing to join the party in power, but he remained in Florence until well after the end of World War II, during which conflict he managed to escape harassment. The Florence years bore rich fruit. There, Montale was at the center of "Hermeticism," the literary movement taking shape around his, Ungaretti's, and, later, Quasimodo's leading work. In fastidious Florence, they still remember the part Montale had in the lively literary meetings at the cafés the "Giubbe Rosse" and the "Paskowski."

In 1932 he published *La casa dei doganieri e altri versi* (The Customs-House and Other Verse), which was incorporated in 1939 in *Le Occasioni* (The Occasions), an epoch-making book as prophetic of the disaster impending over Europe and the world at large as the first book had been commemorative in its way of the earlier war's consequences. The signs of the gathering storm appear lucidly in the poem "Eastbourne," where the local Bank Holiday implies merely an uneasy lull in the unceasing fight of "unarmed goodness" against "conquering evil"; likewise, a poem occasioned by another European landscape, "Boats on the Marne," symbolically envisages the loss of mankind's great aboriginal hope — the dream of justice and happiness — in the flow of the river plied by Sunday oarsmen. The festive appearances are deceptive.

This time the impact on the Italian literary world proved massive, not spare as it had been with *Ossi di Seppia*, for many things had happened in the intervening fourteen years: Montale's endorsement by critics of Emilio Cecchi's caliber, a first literary prize in 1932, and the growth of a readership responsive to his message of human dignity. His appeal was broadly ethical and stylistic, rather than just political, and he spoke for all those youths who sensed the fatal disarray of their world and kept looking for redemptive signs on the eve of war. *Le Occasioni* is as deeply searching a book as its title is modest, and it marks a sharp concentration of language.

The poet himself claims that his prophecy had been an easy one for a man alert to the omens of the time, and the prophecy became explicit diagnosis in 1942, when he published *Finisterre* at Lugano, Switzerland, and retrospectively even more so in 1956, when the Venetian publisher, Neri Pozza, issued in a limited edition *La Bufera e Altro* (The Storm and Other Things), Montale's third major book of verse. Like the rest of Montale's work, *La Bufera* (which incorporates *Finisterre)*, was then reissued by Mondadori, the Milan publisher to whom Montale acted as consultant.

Since 1948, Montale has made his home in Milan, where he still lives and works as a contributing editor of the literary section of *Il Corriere della Sera*, the influential daily to whose night edition he also contributes chronicles of musical events. This least melodramatic of Italian writers likes opera and operetta, and at one time he even had voice training for *bel canto*. If mention of his other interests can add anything to the understanding of his poetic personality, it will not be inappropriate to say that he cultivates painting as an amateur; the delicately subdued tones of his small landscapes are reminiscent of the chromatic key of his poetry. This whole side of him also reflects the light touch which often counterpoints the gravity of his verse.

There is no ignoring the lightness (at times even whimsy) of certain *Bufera* poems, and no underrating the gravity of *Satura* (1962), an informally published collection of five poems. The more sustained of these, "Botta e Riposta" (Thrust and Riposte), epitomizes allegorically the spiritual career of a man who was appalled by Fascist dictatorship only to be disappointed afterward by what he considers the failure of postwar Italy to live up to the promise of its liberation. Thus the only attitude possible to him is one of watchful disengagement. He sees no real distinction between tyranny and mass conformity, and he refuses to surrender his dream of personal dignity. Unwelcome as the message may sound to committed, or just hopeful, ears, it is consistent with the poet's lifelong struggle to be himself in the teeth of whatever threats or inducements. The narrative allegory in this poem from *Satura* picks up the Kafkaesque cue of "Il Prigioniero" (The Prisoner) at the end of the *Bufera* volume, and, ideological interest apart, neither poem is immune from a certain stylistic slackness. This flaw, however, is absent from a related piece which immediately precedes "The Prisoner" in *La Bufera*: "Piccolo Testamento" (Little Testament), forcefully voicing Montale's political pessimism, is as moving as anything he ever wrote.

Even a cursory survey of Montale's published work would remain glaringly incomplete without mention of two booklets which comprise material dating respectively from his Florentine and from his Milanese period: the *Quaderno di traduzioni* (Copybook of Translations) of 1948 and the *Farfalla di Dinard* (Butterfly of Dinard) of 1956. Though not so prominently a translator of poetry as Ezra Pound, Montale has done work in this area which bears scrutiny, if only because he applied to the Italian rendition of his foreign texts the same care he invests in the transcription of the dictates of his own inner voice. The authors chosen for translation include the Shakespeare of the sonnets, Thomas Hardy, T. S. Eliot, G. M. Hopkins, Emily Dickinson, Herman Melville, among others. The *Farfalla di Dinard* is a collection of thin prose sketches previously published by the Milan newspaper which employs him, their anecdotal tone linking them plausibly enough to make a book. They are mostly something between the short story and the autobiographical essay, yet their casualness often veils something deeper; the author himself says that some of them, including the title piece, are closely related to his early poetry. Witticism may disguise epiphany, and then we have telling, if unpretentious, prose poems on Montale's major themes. Two such writings found their way into the pages of *La Bufera*.

It is unlikely that major additions will come to alter the essential physiognomy of Montale's work as we now have it. The three main phases, identifiable with *Ossi di Seppia*, *Le Occasioni*, and *La Bufera*, cohere in a cycle of poetical creativity which it is by now possible to see in perspective. If we keep in mind that the first unrejected poem dates from 1916, while the latest published ones appeared in 1962, that cycle spans almost half a century, through the experiences of two world wars bridged by a dictatorial interlude. The commonplace, "poetry of crisis," obviously applies to Montale's verse, but if it were only that, it would have too much competition to deserve an eminent place in the international arena. There is art that simply registers crisis, and there is art that meets it victoriously. Montale's poetry is of the latter kind, and I would call it not so much a poetry of crisis as a poetry of fidelity. Fidelity to unadulterated existence, to memory, to love; fidelity to language—and at a time when none of these values can be taken for granted any more. To read *Ossi di Seppia* is to appreciate the scrupulous care he has brought to the Italian language, his attentive pondering of each syllable's color, of each word's specific weight, of each phrase's dynamism. To read *Le Occasioni* and the best of *La Bufera* is to realize how much nonchalance this devotee of precision can afford.

Such ease of diction was just as much a personal conquest as it was a gift. The zest of pre-World War I avantgarde schools in Italy had cleared the ground of much academic rubbish, but their ferments had also engendered confusion. D'Annunzio's rhetoric receded into the past, and the present was disputed by the ephemeral Futurist iconoclasts and the demure *Crepuscolari* practitioners of a "twilight" bourgeois poetry centering on the intimacy of the quotidian. Neither of those schools could do more than point the way to a firmer accomplishment, and this came signally with Ungaretti and Montale, though we should not discount Montale's avowed debt to Gozzano, the leading *Crepuscolare*. Parallel as it was in its long-range effects, Montale's and Ungaretti's intervention took place in opposite ways, for the Egyptian-born and French-educated Ungaretti began by breaking totally with traditional prosody and vocabulary, while the Ligurian provincial from Genoa strove to retain as much as possible of the inherited patterns. His renewal of poetical language was conducted from inside the tradition; one will notice that most of the *Ossi di Seppia* poems, and many in the following volumes, cling to received rhythm and meter. Another noticeable trait that sets off Montale from the earliest Ungaretti is the former's use of a richer lexical range, including several decidedly literary words for which one would comb in vain Ungaretti's first writing.

And yet, the total effect in Montale's case is not one of preciosity, but of sharp delineation. One always senses that the rare word is there for the sake of functional focus, not of showiness, for it is effortlessly absorbed in the stylistic organism, thanks to a clever balance of phrasing. From the start, Montale tends to be a poet of supple, abundant syntax; Ungaretti, a poet of suspended images. Montale, of course, was to prove increasingly capable of elliptical compression, while his rival developed in the direction of syntactical complexity. For all that, what Montale mainly did to Italian poetry was to introduce a conversational style which would not be doomed to drab conversation. The American reader will here remember the comparable revolution staged by Pound, Eliot, and Marianne Moore, and in his own quiet way by Frost, against late-Victorian pomp or singsong. To lower the basic tone meant, in each case, to make a deeper, subtler music possible; the operation was more urgently needed for a language like Italian, which had been so persistently hypnotized by its own native melody. On the other hand, see to what ecstatic pitch Montale can unobtrusively rise with "Portami il Girasole" (Bring Me the Sunflower): no one could claim here that the option for a chastened idiom has precluded the possibility of heightened vision. His understated verse is punctuated by lightnings.

Technical expertise is enlisted in the service of an apocalyptic writing. Montale can use rhyme traditionally, or he can do without it, or vary it by assonance, or muffle it by removing it to the middle of a line — a device he learned from that other austere poet, Leopardi. As to the rhythm: the Italian line typically being the hendecasyllable (as iambic pentameter is in English), Montale can tone it down by enjambement, by run-on lines, and he can loosen it by occasionally injecting an extra syllable. A careful distribution of pauses in the body of the verse contributes to rhythmical resilience, and the tactical employment of alliteration makes the lines crepitate and jerk where the expressive value demanded is rhythmic resistance rather than an even flow. There are rapids and cataracts in the river of this verse. The harsh, dense sounds of "Meriggiare," for instance, are percussive, not melodic. Montale found an illustrious model for this technique in Dante's "rime pietrose" (stony rimes for Lady Pietra) and, generally, in Dante's "rime aspre" (harsh rimes) of *Inferno*.

Such a technical affinity, which matches the Dantesque severity of so many landscapes and situations in Montale, has rightly reminded a few readers of Eliot's wasteland poetry; yet Montale exhibits also some quite un-Eliotic traits, and it is impossible to reduce him to one such counterpart. One could hardly find in Eliot the insistent note of love for an absent lady which marks Montale as a kind of modern troubadour. "Dora Markus" is one of the most poignant love elegies of all time, and "L'orto" (The Garden) raises love to a transfiguring worship. Already the pervasiveness of her elusive presence in the hauntingly brief "Mottetti" makes the exotic lady a kind of glimpsed godhead. Then there are the more terrene, if equally tender, addresses to a present lady in *La Bufera*.

Soberly modern, yet polemically anachronistic like Yeats; disenchanted, but capable of affectionate hyperboles; increasingly elliptical and allusive to the verge of obscurity, though all the while impelled by an unrelenting will to incisive clarity, and occasionally prone to effusive eloquence, or to poignant levity: such a writer escapes comfortable definitions. No critical formula can capture the essence of Eugenio Montale's poetry, whose appeal to a sharpened sensibility has durably changed the poetical situation of Italy. Europe speaks in many tongues; through Montale Italy has added one more unforgettable voice to the European, or we should say Western, concert.

To echo, transpose, or emulate this voice in English is a hard task, perhaps an impossible one, yet the translations by several authors, as sampled in the present volume, may satisfy the most exacting tastes. Many American and British poets have been responding to the challenge of Montale's texts, and it was not easy to choose among the available versions. In some instances it seemed advisable to offer more than one translation of the same poem. One flame can be refracted through different crystals, one music transcribed for diverse instruments. It is to be hoped that all the translations in this book will stand on their own merits as English poems, at the same time helping many readers to gain easier access to the severe music and sudden light of the Italian originals.

THE TRANSLATORS

Ben Belitt
Irma Brandeis
Glauco Cambon
Cid Corman
Maurice English
G. S. Fraser
George Kay
Robert Lowell
James Merrill
John Frederick Nims
Alfredo de Palchi
Mario Praz
Sonia Raiziss
Vinio Rossi
Charles Wright
David P. Young

OSSI DI SEPPIA

CUTTLEFISH BONES

I LIMONI

Ascoltami, i poeti laureati
si muovono soltanto fra le piante
dai nomi poco usati: bossi ligustri o acanti.
Io, per me, amo le strade che riescono agli erbosi
fossi dove in pozzanghere
mezzo seccate agguantano i ragazzi
qualche sparuta anguilla:
le viuzze che seguono i ciglioni,
discendono tra i ciuffi delle canne
e mettono negli orti, tra gli alberi dei limoni.

Meglio se le gazzarre degli uccelli
si spengono inghiottite dall'azzurro:
piú chiaro si ascolta il susurro
dei rami amici nell'aria che quasi non si muove,
e i sensi di quest'odore
che non sa staccarsi da terra
e piove in petto una dolcezza inquieta.
Qui delle divertite passioni
per miracolo tace la guerra,
qui tocca anche a noi poveri la nostra parte di ricchezza
ed è l'odore dei limoni.

Vedi, in questi silenzi in cui le cose
s'abbandonano e sembrano vicine
a tradire il loro ultimo segreto,

THE LEMON TREES

Listen; the poets laureate
walk only among plants
of unfamiliar name: boxwood, acanthus;
I, for my part, prefer the streets that fade
to grassy ditches where a boy
hunting the half-dried puddles
sometimes scoops up a meagre eel;
the little paths that wind along the slopes,
plunge down among the cane-tufts,
and break into the orchards, among trunks
   of the lemon-trees.
Better if the jubilee of birds
is quenched, swallowed entirely in the blue:
more clear to the listener murmur of friendly
   boughs
in air that scarcely moves,
that fills the senses with this odor
inseparable from earth,
and rains an unquiet sweetness in the breast.
Here by a miracle is hushed
the war of the diverted passions,
here even to us poor falls our share of riches,
and it is the scent of the lemon-trees.

See, in these silences
in which things yield and seem
about to betray their ultimate secret,

talora ci si aspetta
di scoprire uno sbaglio di Natura,
il punto morto del mondo, l'anello che non tiene,
il filo da disbrogliare che finalmente ci metta
nel mezzo di una verità.
Lo sguardo fruga d'intorno,
la mente indaga accorda disunisce
nel profumo che dilaga
quando il giorno piú languisce.
Sono i silenzi in cui si vede
in ogni ombra umana che si allontana
qualche disturbata Divinità.

Ma l'illusione manca e ci riporta il tempo
nelle città rumorose dove l'azzurro si mostra
soltanto a pezzi, in alto, tra le cimase.
La pioggia stanca la terra, di poi; s'affolta
il tedio dell'inverno sulle case,
la luce si fa avara – amara l'anima.
Quando un giorno da un malchiuso portone
tra gli alberi di una corte
ci si mostrano i gialli dei limoni;
e il gelo del cuore si sfa,
e in petto ci scrosciano
le loro canzoni
le trombe d'oro della solarità.

sometimes one half expects
to discover a mistake of Nature,
the dead point of the world, the link which
    will not hold,
the thread to disentangle which might set us
    at last
in the midst of a truth.
The eyes cast round,
the mind seeks harmonizes disunites
in the perfume that expands
when day most languishes.
Silences in which one sees
in each departing human shadow
some dislodged Divinity.
But the illusion wanes and time returns us
to our clamorous cities where the blue
    appears
only in patches, high up, among the gables.
Then rain falls wearying the earth,
the winter tedium weighs on the roofs,
the light grows miserly, bitter the soul.
When one day through a half-shut gate,
among the leafage of a court
the yellows of the lemon blaze
and the heart's ice melts
and songs
pour into the breast
from golden trumpets of solarity.

                                        [I. B.]

QUASI UNA FANTASIA

Raggiorna, lo presento
da un albore di frusto
argento alle pareti:
lista un barlume le finestre chiuse.
Torna l'avvenimento
del sole e le diffuse
voci, i consueti strepiti non porta.

Perché? Penso ad un giorno d'incantesimo
e delle giostre d'ore troppo uguali
mi ripago. Traboccherà la forza
che mi turgeva, incosciente mago,
da grande tempo. Ora m'affaccerò,
subisserò alte case, spogli viali.

Avrò di contro un paese d'intatte nevi
ma lievi come viste in un arazzo.
Scivolerà dal cielo bioccoso un tardo raggio.
Gremite d'invisibile luce selve e colline
mi diranno l'elogio degl'ilari ritorni.

Lieto leggerò i neri
segni dei rami sul bianco
come un essenziale alfabeto.

ALMOST A FANTASY

Dawn flows back, its intimation
Touches me from the dull
Silver shining on the walls;
It lays its stripes of light on the closed
    windows.
The advent of the sun
Recurs, but not
The accustomed din, the scattered morning
    voices.

Thinking of a day of enchantment,
From the ferris-wheel of equal turning hours
I slip away.
Time has ripened in me, unwitting wizard,
Power which must pour itself out.
Now I will fling the window wide,
Blot out the high houses and the empty
    streets.

I will shape for my feet a land of stainless
    snow
Bland as a snowscape in a tapestry,
With a late glowing in the fleecy sky.
Ripe with invisible light, forests and hills
Will utter the praise of every glad renewal.
And gladly I will read
Like an alphabet of the absolute
The tracing of the branches black on white.

Tutto il passato in un punto
dinanzi mi sarà comparso.
Non turberà suono alcuno
quest'allegrezza solitaria.
Filerà nell'aria
o scenderà s'un paletto
qualche galletto di marzo.

CAFFÈ A RAPALLO

Natale nel tepidario
lustrante, truccato dai fumi
che svolgono tazze, velato
tremore di lumi oltre i chiusi
cristalli, profili di femmine
nel grigio, tra lampi di gemme
e screzi di sete...
                Son giunte
a queste native tue spiagge,
le nuove Sirene!; e qui manchi
Camillo, amico, tu storico
di cupidige e di brividi.

S'ode grande frastuono nella via.

È passata di fuori
l'indicibile musica
delle trombe di lama
e dei piattini arguti dei fanciulli:
è passata la musica innocente.

All the past in one moment
Will compose its pageant before my eyes.
No sound whatever will trouble
That solitary happiness.
There will ride through the air
Or glide to rest on a pole
Some random cock of Spring.

[M. E.]

CAFÉ AT RAPALLO

Christmas in the tepidarium,
gleaming, masked by fumes
rising from cups, veiled trembling
of lights beyond the closed
panes, profiles of women
in the dusk rayed through by gems
and whispering silks. . .

            They are come
to these your native beaches,
the new Sirens! And you are wanted here,
Camillo, friend, chronicler
of shudderings and desires.
We hear great fanfare in the street.
Out there has gone by
the unutterable music
of tin horns and of children's cymbals.
This innocent music has gone by.

Un mondo gnomo ne andava
con strepere di muletti e di carriole,
tra un lagno di montoni
di cartapesta e un bagliare
di sciabole fasciate di stagnole.
Passarono i Generali
con le feluche di cartone
e impugnavano aste di torroni;
poi furono i gregari
con moccoli e lampioni,
e le tinnanti scatole
ch'ànno il suono piú trito,
tenue rivo che incanta
l'animo dubitoso:
(meraviglioso udivo).
L'orda passò col rumore
d'una zampante greggia
che il tuono recente impaura.
L'accolse la pastura
che per noi piú non verdeggia.

Non chiederci la parola che squadri da ogni lato
l'animo nostro informe, e a lettere di fuoco
lo dichiari e risplenda come un croco
perduto in mezzo a un polveroso prato.

A gnomish world went with it:
clatter of mules and carts,
a bleating of papier-maché
rams, and a glinting
of sabers sheeted in tinfoil.
By went the Generals
in their cardboard hats,
brandishing spears of nougat;
and then the simple soldiers
with tapers and lanterns
and the little rattles shaken
to produce the tritest of sounds,
tenuous stream that enchants
the doubting mind
(marvelling to my ears).
The crowd went by with the din
of a stampeding herd
that nearby thunder routs.
And pastures welcome them
such as for us no more are green.

[I. B. and J. M.]

TWISTED OF BRIAR

Do not seek here such words as dress and shield
the formless soul; nor the glittering phrase
to speak its splendors forth, as the sun's rays
make flame the crocus in the dusty field.

11

Ah l'uomo che se ne va sicuro,
agli altri ed a se stesso amico,
e l'ombra sua non cura che la canicola
stampa sopra uno scalcinato muro!

Non domandarci la formula che mondi possa aprirti
sí qualche storta sillaba e secca come un ramo.
Codesto solo oggi possiamo dirti,
ciò che *non* siamo, ciò che *non* vogliamo.

Meriggiare pallido e assorto
presso un rovente muro d'orto,
ascoltare tra i pruni e gli sterpi
schiocchi di merli, frusci di serpi.

Nelle crepe del suolo o su la veccia
spiar le file di rosse formiche
ch'ora si rompono ed ora s'intrecciano
a sommo di minuscole biche.

Osservare tra frondi il palpitare
lontano di scaglie di mare
mentre si levano tremuli scricchi
di cicale dai calvi picchi.

— Ah, he who strides forth superb, to all
a friend, his fellows and himself alike,
and has no care that the raging noondays strike
his shadow athwart the length of a crumbling
   wall!

To summon back the old, enchanting days
no spell is hidden here.
                    Arid, twisted of briar,
a few difficult syllables wish only to say
what we are *not*, what we do *not* desire.

                                        [M. E.]

THE WALL

To lie in shadow on the lawn
By a crumbling wall, pale and withdrawn,
And spy in the weeds the gliding snake
And hear the rustle blackbirds make —

To watch in the cracked earth and the grass
Battalions of red ants at drill,
That break and form ranks, pass and repass
In busy marches on some tiny hill —

To catch, each time the leaves blow free,
The faint and pulsing motion of the sea,
While ceaseless, tremulous and shrill,
The cicadas chatter on the bald hill —

E andando nel sole che abbaglia
sentire con triste meraviglia
com'è tutta la vita e il suo travaglio
in questo seguitare una muraglia
che ha in cima cocci aguzzi di bottiglia.

Portami il girasole ch'io lo trapianti
nel mio terreno bruciato dal salino,
e mostri tutto il giorno agli azzurri specchianti
del cielo l'ansietà del suo volto giallino.

Tendono alla chiarità le cose oscure,
si esauriscono i corpi in un fluire
di tinte: queste in musiche. Svanire
è dunque la ventura delle venture.

Portami tu la pianta che conduce
dove sorgono bionde trasparenze
e vapora la vita quale essenza;
portami il girasole impazzito di luce.

Rising, to wander in bewilderment
With the sun's dazzle, and the sorry thought
How all our life, and all its labors spent,
Are like a man upon a journey sent
Along a wall that's sheer and steep and
    endless, dressed
With bits of broken bottles on its crest.

[M. E.]

THE SUNFLOWER

Bring me the sunflower to plant in my garden here
Where the salt of the flung spray has parched
    a space,
And all day long to the blue and mirroring air
Let it turn the ardor of its yellow face.

These dark things to the source of brightness turn,
In a flow of colors into music flowing, spend
Themselves forever. Thus to burn
Is consummation, of all ends the end.

Bring me within your hands that flower
    which yearns
Up to the ultimate transparent white
Where all of life into its essence burns:
Bring me that flower impassioned of the light.

[M. E.]

Portovenere

Là fuoresce il Tritone
dai flutti che lambiscono
le soglie d'un cristiano
tempio, ed ogni ora prossima
è antica. Ogni dubbiezza
si conduce per mano
come una fanciulletta amica.

Là non è chi si guardi
o stia di sé in ascolto.
Quivi sei alle origini
e decidere è stolto:
ripartirai piú tardi
per assumere un volto.

Sul muro grafito
che adombra i sedili rari
l'arco del cielo appare
finito.

Chi si ricorda piú del fuoco ch'arse
impetuoso

PORTOVENERE

There leaps the Triton
out of waves that graze
the threshold of a christian shrine,
and every nearest hour
is old. Every uncertainty
lends you its hand,
as docile as a friendly child.

There no one's eyes and ears
are bent on self.
You stand at origins and can see
decision ill becomes the place.
You will leave presently
in order to assume a face.

[I. B.]

ABOVE THE SCRIBBLED WALL

Above the scribbled wall
shading some stray benches
the arch of the sky seems
closed.

Who remembers the wildfire any more
    that streamed
impetuously

nelle vene del mondo; – in un riposo
freddo le forme, opache, sono sparse.

Rivedrò domani le banchine
e la muraglia e l'usata strada.
Nel futuro che s'apre le mattine
sono ancorate come barche in rada.

Antico, sono ubriacato dalla voce
ch'esce dalle tue bocche quando si schiudono
come verdi campane e si ributtano
indietro e si disciolgono.
La casa delle mie estati lontane,
t'era accanto, lo sai,
là nel paese dove il sole cuoce
e annuvolano l'aria le zanzare.
Come allora oggi in tua presenza impietro,
mare, ma non piú degno
mi credo del solenne ammonimento
del tuo respiro. Tu m'hai detto primo
che il piccino fermento
del mio cuore non era che un momento
del tuo; che mi era in fondo
la tua legge rischiosa: esser vasto e diverso

in the world's veins; — now the dull
forms lie scattered in chilly composure.

Tomorrow I'll see the quays again
and the wall and the accustomed road.
In the future that opens up, the mornings
are moored like boats in the harbor.

                              [S. R. and A. de P.]

ANTICO

I'm drunk with that voice
archaic sea,
pouring from your mouths when they gape
like green bells and are shocked
back and dissolved.
The house of my distant summers,
as you know, belonged to you
there in that country of scorching suns
and low air fogged with midges.
Stunned now, as I once was, in your presence
I no longer believe myself worth
the solemn exhortation of your breath.
It was you who first taught me
my heart's puny tumult
was only a moment of yours —
that at bottom I kept your hazardous
law: to be vast and various

e insieme fisso:
e svuotarmi cosí d'ogni lordura
come tu fai che sbatti sulle sponde
tra sugheri alghe asterie
le inutili macerie del tuo abisso.

Avrei voluto sentirmi scabro ed essenziale
siccome i ciottoli che tu volvi,
mangiati dalla salsedine;
scheggia fuori del tempo, testimone
di una volontà fredda che non passa.
Altro fui: uomo intento che riguarda
in sé, in altrui, il bollore
della vita fugace – uomo che tarda
all'atto, che nessuno, poi, distrugge.
Volli cercare il male
che tarla il mondo, la piccola stortura
d'una leva che arresta
l'ordegno universale; e tutti vidi
gli eventi del minuto
come pronti a disgiungersi in un crollo.
Seguíto il solco d'un sentiero m'ebbi
l'opposto in cuore, col suo invito; e forse
m'occorreva il coltello che recide,

yet steady:
and so to purge myself of rubbish
as you do, hurling on the beaches
among starfish corks seaweed
the waste of your abyss.

[S. R. and A. de P.]

ROUGH AND ESSENTIAL

I would have wanted to be rough and
    essential
as the pebbles you turn over
gnawed by the sea salt;
a splinter outside time, witness
to a cold perpetual will.
No, I was a man intent on
watching the transient bubbling of life
in himself, in others — a man who delays
action, that no one then destroys.
I wanted to search out the evil
that bores through the world, the lever's
slight flaw locking the gears
of the universe: and I saw all
the events of the minute as though
poised to crash in a downpour of pieces.
In the wake of one road I took
the opposite offer to heart; and maybe
I needed the knife that cuts clean,

la mente che decide e si determina.
Altri libri occorrevano
a me, non la tua pagina rombante.
Ma nulla so rimpiangere: tu sciogli
ancora i groppi interni col tuo canto.
Il tuo delirio sale agli astri ormai.

Dissipa tu se lo vuoi
questa debole vita che si lagna,
come la spugna il frego
effimero di una lavagna.
M'attendo di ritornare nel tuo circolo,
s'adempia lo sbandato mio passare.
La mia venuta era testimonianza
di un ordine che in viaggio mi scordai,
giurano fede queste mie parole
a un evento impossibile, e lo ignorano.
Ma sempre che traudii
la tua dolce risacca su le prode
sbigottimento mi prese
quale d'uno scemato di memoria
quando si risovviene del suo paese.
Presa la mia lezione

the clenched mind that chooses.
The text I needed was not
your roaring page.
But I regret nothing: again you
undo the inward tangle with your talk.
And now your delirium climbs starward.

[S. R. and A. de P.]

DISSOLVE IT, IF YOU WISH

This little crying life —
dissolve it, if you wish,
as a sponge from a blackboard
wipes an ephemeral scrawl.
My own foundering voyage done,
I wait to return within your circuiting.
My very coming was testimony
to an order which in travelling I had
    forgotten,
these very words of mine have pledged
    a blind faith
to a consummation which is not to be.
But whenever I have faintly heard
the soft pulsations of your surf
consternation has seized hold of me
as when memory blurs for a man
trying to recall the landscape of his youth.
Much from your savage exultation

piú che dalla tua gloria
aperta, dall'ansare
che quasi non dà suono
di qualche tuo meriggio desolato,
a te mi rendo in umiltà. Non sono
che favilla d'un tirso. Bene lo so: bruciare,
questo, non altro, è il mio significato.

ARSENIO

I turbini sollevano la polvere
sui tetti, a mulinelli, e sugli spiazzi
deserti, ove i cavalli incappucciati
annusano la terra, fermi innanzi
ai vetri luccicanti degli alberghi.
Sul corso, in faccia al mare, tu discendi
in questo giorno
or piovorno ora acceso, in cui par scatti
a sconvolgerne l'ore
uguali, strette in trama, un ritornello
di castagnette.

È il segno d'un'altra orbita: tu seguilo.
Discendi all'orizzonte che sovrasta
una tromba di piombo, alta sui gorghi,

I have learned my wisdom, and much more
from that still flame
which burns and makes no sound,
your long and desolate and noonday trance.
Humbly I give myself to you. A spark
for the great burning. This burning, well
    I know,
and this alone, is my significance.

                                                    [M. E.]

ARSENIO
To G. B. Angioletti

Dust, dust is blown about the roofs, in
    eddies;
It eddies on the roofs and on the places
Deserted, where are seen the hoodéd horses
Sniffing the ground, motionless
In front of the glistening lattices of the hotels.
Along the promenade, facing the sea, you slide,
Upon this afternoon of sun and rain,
Whose even, close-knit, hours
Are shattered, so it seems, now and again
By a snappy refrain
Of castanets.

Sign of an alien orbit: follow it.
Then slide ye towards the horizon, overhung
By a leaden waterspout, high o'er the waves,

piú d'essi vagabonda: salso nembo
vorticante, soffiato dal ribelle
elemento alle nubi; fa che il passo
su la ghiaia ti scricchioli e t'inciampi
il viluppo dell'alghe: quell'istante
è forse, molto atteso, che ti scampi
dal finire il tuo viaggio, anello d'una
catena, immoto andare, oh troppo noto
delirio, Arsenio, d'immobilità...

Ascolta tra i palmizi il getto tremulo
dei violini, spento quando rotola
il tuono con un fremer di lamiera
percossa; la tempesta è dolce quando
sgorga bianca la stella di Canicola
nel cielo azzurro e lunge par la sera
ch'è prossima: se il fulmine la incide
dirama come un albero prezioso
entro la luce che s'arrosa: e il timpano
degli tzigani è il rombo silenzioso.

Discendi in mezzo al buio che precipita
e muta il mezzogiorno in una notte

More restless than the waves: a briny
   whirlwind
Spumed of the unruly element 'gainst
   the clouds;
Tread on the rustling shingle,
And let your foot be trammelled by the weeds:
Maybe, your journey needs
This very moment, this long wished for
   moment,
To be saved from an end:
Your journey — link of an eternal chain —
A motion motionless, Arsenio, a too
   well-known
Delirious stir of immobility.

Listen, among the palm-trees, to the
   tremulous spray
Of violins, quenchéd when the thunder rolls
Clanging like many smitten iron plates:
Sweet is the tempest when in the blue sky
White rushes out the dog-star, and Eventide,
Which is so close at hand, seems still so far;
The thunderbolt, when splitting it, forth
   branches,
A precious tree within a rosy light.
The Tziganies' timbals are the silent rumble.

Along you slide, 'midst the precipitous
   darkness
Turning the noon into some strange midnight

di globi accesi, dondolanti a riva, –
e fuori, dove un'ombra sola tiene
mare e cielo, dai gozzi sparsi palpita
l'acetilene –

finché goccia trepido
il cielo, fuma il suolo che s'abbevera,
tutto d'accanto ti sciaborda, sbattono
le tende molli, un frúscio immenso rade
la terra, giú s'afflosciano stridendo
le lanterne di carta sulle strade.

Cosí sperso tra i vimini e le stuoie
grondanti, giunco tu che le radici
con sé trascina, viscide, non mai
svelte, tremi di vita e ti protendi
a un vuoto risonante di lamenti
soffocati, la tesa ti ringhiotte
dell'onda antica che ti volge; e ancora
tutto che ti riprende, strada portico
mura specchi ti figge in una sola
ghiacciata moltitudine di morti,
e se un gesto ti sfiora, una parola
ti cade accanto, quello è forse, Arsenio,
nell'ora che si scioglie, il cenno d'una
vita strozzata per te sorta, e il vento
la porta con la cenere degli astri.

Of kindled globes, whose oscillation spreads
Over the beach; and over distant places,
Where sky and sea melt into a solid shadow,
From scattered boats white throbs the
    acetylene –

Until the sky gives out in trembling drops,
The dank soil steams, everything, close by,
Is o'erflowed, the drenchéd tents are flapping,
An immense flurry skims the earth;
    down hurled
Rustle the paper lanterns on the streets.

So, lost among the wickers and the mats
Dripping, you, reed that drags along its roots
Clammy, never torn up, you shake with life,
You stretch yourself towards a resounding void
Of choked laments; the dome of the ancient wave
Swallows you up again, revolves you; again
All that takes you, street, porch, walls,
    mirrors, nails you

To a lonely, icy multitude of dead.
And should a gesture touch you, should
    a word
Fall at your side, such is perhaps, Arsenio,
In the dissolving hour, the lost appeal
Of some strangled life which rose for you;
    the wind
Carries it off with the ashes of the stars.

                                    [M. P.]

CRISALIDE

L'albero verdecupo
si stria di giallo tenero e s'ingromma.
Vibra nell'aria una pietà per l'avide
radici, per le tumide cortecce.
Son vostre queste piante
scarse che si rinnovano
all'alito d'Aprile, umide e liete.
Per me che vi contemplo da quest'ombra,
altro cespo riverdica, e voi siete.

Ogni attimo vi porta nuove fronde
e il suo sbigottimento avanza ogni altra
gioia fugace; viene a impetuose onde
la vita a questo estremo angolo d'orto.
Lo sguardo ora vi cade su le zolle;
una risacca di memorie giunge
al vostro cuore e quasi lo sommerge.
Lunge risuona un grido: ecco precipita
il tempo, spare con risucchi rapidi
tra i sassi, ogni ricordo è spento; ed io
dall'oscuro mio canto mi protendo
a codesto solare avvenimento.

Voi non pensate ciò che vi rapiva
come oggi, allora, il tacito compagno

CHRYSALIS

The sombre-green tree
streaks with tender yellow and encrusts.
In the air a pity quivers for the greedy
roots, for the swollen bark.
These plants are yours, sparse,
that grow new again
at the breath of April, bathed and glad.
For me who watch you from this shadow,
another bush greens again, and, there,
    you are.

Every instant brings you new leaves
and its consternation surpasses every other
short-lived joy; life in sudden waves
comes to this remote garden corner.
Your gaze now falls upon the turf,
a surfing of memory reaches
your heart and almost whelms it.
From far-off echoes a cry: there, time lunges,
disappears with swift eddies
among the stones, every memento is gone,
    and I
from my dark retreat stretch towards
the event there of sun.

You do not imagine what carried away
then, as today, your mute companion

che un meriggio lontano vi portava.
Siete voi la mia preda, che m'offrite
un'ora breve di tremore umano.
Perderne non vorrei neppure un attimo:
è questa la mia parte, ogni altra è vana.
La mia ricchezza è questo sbattimento
che vi trapassa e il viso
in alto vi rivolge; questo lento
giro d'occhi che ormai sanno vedere.

Cosí va la certezza d'un momento
con uno sventolio di tende e di alberi
tra le case; ma l'ombra non dissolve
che vi reclama, opaca. M'apparite
allora, come me, nel limbo squallido
delle monche esistenze; e anche la vostra
rinascita è uno sterile segreto,
un prodigio fallito come tutti
quelli che ci fioriscono d'accanto.

E il flutto che si scopre oltre le sbarre
come ci parla a volte di salvezza;
come può sorgere agile
l'illusione, e sciogliere i suoi fumi.
Vanno a spire sul mare, ora si fondono
sull'orizzonte in foggia di golette.
Spicca una d'esse un volo senza rombo,

whom a distant noon brought you.
My prey you are, offering me
a brief hour of human tremor.
I will not miss even an instant of it:
this is my part, every other is empty.
My wealth is this unrest
that runs you through and turns
your face upwards: this slow
gazing round of eyes which now can see.

So the certainty of a moment goes
with a fluttering of awnings and trees
among the houses, but the shadow
   does not melt
that reclaims you dully. You appear to me
then, like myself, in the sordid limbo
of maimed existences; and even your
rebirth is a barren secret,
an exploded wonder like all
those which flower beside us.

And the flood which shows above
   the barred gate
how it speaks to us at times of salvation;
how nimbly the illusion
can rise and release its smoke clouds.
They go spiralling over the sea,
   now they merge
on the horizon, shaped like schooners.
One of them launches into noiseless flight,

l'acque di piombo come alcione profugo
rade. Il sole s'immerge nelle nubi,
l'ora di febbre, trepida, si chiude.
Un glorioso affanno senza strepiti
ci batte in gola: nel meriggio afoso
spunta la barca di salvezza, è giunta:
vedila che sciaborda tra le secche,
esprime un suo burchiello che si volge
al docile frangente – e là ci attende.

Ah crisalide, com'è amara questa
tortura senza nome che ci volve
e ci porta lontani – e poi non restano
neppure le nostre orme sulla polvere;
e noi andremo innanzi senza smuovere
un sasso solo della gran muraglia;
e forse tutto è fisso, tutto è scritto,
e non vedremo sorgere per via
la libertà, il miracolo,
il fatto che non era necessario!

Nell'onda e nell'azzurro non è scia.
Sono mutati i segni della proda
dianzi raccolta come un dolce grembo.
Il silenzio ci chiude nel suo lembo
e le labbra non s'aprono per dire
il patto ch'io vorrei
stringere col destino: di scontare

shears the leaden waters like a refugee
sea-gull. The sun goes under cloud,
the fever hour, tremulous, is ending.
A glorious fatigue without outcry
beats in our throats: in the sultry noon
the boat of salvation heaves in sight, arrives:
see it there as it foams between the banks,
it sends out a long-boat which turns
in the mild breakers—and
     there it waits for us.

Ah chrysalis, how bitter
this nameless torture that besets us
and carries us far—and then not even
our footprints to be left in the dust;
and we shall go on without shifting
a stone, a single one, in the great wall;
and perhaps everything is fixed,
     everything is written,
and we shall not see rising on our way
liberty, the miracle,
the event that was no necessity!

On the wave and on the blue no wake is seen.
The signs have altered on the beach,
before, it was gathered like a pleasant lap.
Silence locks us in its cloud
and lips do not part to speak
the pact that I would
seal with destiny: to pay for

la vostra gioia con la mia condanna.
Ê il voto che mi nasce ancora in petto,
poi finirà ogni moto. Penso allora
alle tacite offerte che sostengono
le case dei viventi; al cuore che abdica
perché rida un fanciullo inconsapevole;
al taglio netto che recide, al rogo
morente che s'avviva
d'un arido paletto, e ferve trepido.

I MORTI

Il mare che si frange sull'opposta
riva vi leva un nembo che spumeggia
finché la piana lo riassorbe. Quivi
gettammo un dí su la ferrigna costa,
ansante piú del pelago la nostra
speranza! – e il gorgo sterile verdeggia
come ai dí che ci videro fra i vivi.

Or che aquilone spiana il groppo torbido
delle salse correnti e le rivolge
d'onde trassero, attorno alcuno appende
ai rami cedui reti dilunganti
sul viale che discende
oltre lo sguardo;

your joy with my being condemned.
It is the prayer that still wakes in my heart,
then every motion will cease. I think now
of the unworded offerings which prop
the houses of the living; of the heart
   which renounces
so that a child, unknowing, may laugh;
of the clean cut which severs, of the dying
bonfire that flares again
with a dried-up stake and blazes tremblingly.
                           [G. K.]

THE DEAD

The sea crashing on the opposite shore
heaves up a cloud that foams
until the flats absorb it. There
one time on the iron coast we hurled
wilder than the ocean, our hardbreathing
hope! — and the barren vortex turns
green as in days that saw us still living.

Now that the north wind levels the sullen
tangle of salt tides and whips them back
where they reared, someone nearby throws
nets over the brushwood, uncoiling
along the roadway that sinks
out of sight;

reti stinte che asciuga il tocco tardo
e freddo della luce; e sopra queste
denso il cristallo dell'azzurro palpebra
e precipita a un arco d'orizzonte
flagellato.
        Piú d'alga che trascini
il ribollio che a noi si scopre, muove
tale sosta la nostra vita: turbina
quanto in noi rassegnato a' suoi confini
risté un giorno; tra i fili che congiungono
un ramo all'altro si dibatte il cuore
come la gallinella
di mare che s'insacca tra le maglie;
e immobili e vaganti ci ritiene
una fissità gelida.
        Cosí
forse anche ai morti è tolto ogni riposo
nelle zolle: una forza indi li tragge
spietata piú del vivere, ed attorno,
larve rimorse dai ricordi umani,
li volge fino a queste spiagge, fiati
senza materia o voce
traditi dalla tenebra; ed i mozzi
loro voli ci sfiorano pur ora
da noi divisi appena e nel crivello
del mare si sommergono...

bleached nets dried by the slow
chill touch of the light; and above them
the thick lens of the sky blinks
and drops to a curve of the flogged
horizon.
        Deeper than seaweed that drags
in the eddy disclosed to us, our life is
troubled by this lull: whatever once stopped
in us, resigned to its cage
still swirls; between strands that link
one branch to the next, the heart fights
like a marsh hen
trapped in the meshes;
and a freezing deadlock holds us
rigid and wandering.
                So too
perhaps the dead in the sod are denied
any rest: from there a force more ruthless
than life pulls them, and all round
the ghosts reproached by human reminders
are driven as far as these beaches, breaths
without substance or sound
betrayed by the darkness; and their cropped
flights hardly cut off from us now
skim by and in the sieve
of the sea go under. . .

                        [S. R. and A. de P.]

LE OCCASIONI

THE OCCASIONS

LINDAU

La rondine vi porta
fili d'erba, non vuole che la vita passi.
Ma tra gli argini, a notte, l'acqua morta
logora i sassi.
Sotto le torce fumicose sbanda
sempre qualche ombra sulle prode vuote.
Nel cerchio della piazza una sarabanda
s'agita al mugghio dei battelli a ruote.

BAGNI DI LUCCA

Fra il tonfo dei marroni
e il gemito del torrente
che uniscono i loro suoni
ésita il cuore.

Precoce inverno che borea
abbrividisce. M'affaccio
sul ciglio che scioglie l'albore
del giorno nel ghiaccio.

Marmi, rameggi –
           e ad uno scrollo giú
foglie a élice, a freccia,
nel fossato.

LINDAU

The swallow, that life may not fail,
comes there with his grass-blade.
But over the jetties at night a dead water
wears through the shale.
Always in torch-smoke
the darkness divides on the void of the
    shore-line.
In the round of the plaza a sarabande
stirs: the wheels of the paddle-boats wail.

[B. B.]

BAGNI DI LUCCA

Between the thud of the falling chestnuts
And the groan of the torrent
That unite their sounds
The heart hesitates.

Premature winter that the north wind
Shudders through! I present myself
At the ledge which lets loose the twilight
Of the day into the ice.

Marbles, branchings –
                and at a shaking
Leaves in spirals, like arrows,
Into the ditch.

43

Passa l'ultima greggia nella nebbia
del suo fiato.

CAVE D'AUTUNNO

su cui discende la primavera lunare
e nimba di candore ogni frastaglio,
schianti di pigne, abbaglio
di reti stese e schegge,

ritornerà ritornerà sul gelo
la bontà d'una mano,
varcherà il cielo lontano
la ciurma luminosa che ci saccheggia.

A LIUBA CHE PARTE

Non il grillo ma il gatto
del focolare
or ti consiglia, splendido
lare della dispersa tua famiglia.
La casa che tu rechi
con te ravvolta, gabbia o cappelliera?,

44

There passes the last herd, lost in the mist
Of the beasts' own breath.

[G. S. F.]

AUTUMN CELLARS

On which descends the lunar spring,
haloes with light chipped jugs,
cleft pine cones, dazzlement
of drying nets, splinters of wood.

There will return, there will return across
    the frost
the bounty of a hand;
and there will ford the distant sky
again the luminous horde that sacks
    the heart.

[I. B.]

FOR LIUBA, LEAVING

Not now the cricket: the cat
on the hearthstone
will counsel you, magnificent
god of your scattered paternity.
The house that you take with you,
coiled – band-box or bird-cage? –

sovrasta i ciechi tempi come il flutto
arca leggera – e basta al tuo riscatto.

DORA MARKUS

I

Fu dove il ponte di legno
mette a Porto Corsini sul mare alto
e rari uomini, quasi immoti, affondano
o salpano le reti. Con un segno
della mano additavi all'altra sponda
invisibile la tua patria vera.
Poi seguimmo il canale fino alla darsena
della città, lucida di fuliggine,
nella bassura dove s'affondava
una primavera inerte, senza memoria.

E qui dove un'antica vita
si screzia in una dolce
ansietà d'Oriente,
le tue parole iridavano come le scaglie
della triglia moribonda.

La tua irrequietudine mi fa pensare
agli uccelli di passo che urtano ai fari
nelle sere tempestose:
è una tempesta anche la tua dolcezza,

surmounts the blind weathers, buoyantly,
an ark on the torrent,
and will serve for salvation.

[B. B.]

DORA MARKUS

I
It was where the wooden pier juts out
above the sea at Porto Corsini
and a few men, almost immobile, drop
and pull up nets. With a wave
of your hand you pointed at the unseen
land across the sea – your own.
Then we followed the canal
back to the heart of town, shiny with soot,
a flat lowland where paralyzed April
was sinking, empty of memories.

And here where an ancient life
is dappled with a soft
oriental worry,
your words made a rainbow
like the scales on a stranded fish.

Your unrest reminds me
of those great birds of passage
who brain themselves against beacons
during evening storms:
your sweetness itself is a storm

turbina e non appare,
e i suoi riposi sono anche piú rari.
Non so come stremata tu resisti
in questo lago
d'indifferenza ch'è il tuo cuore; forse
ti salva un amuleto che tu tieni
vicino alla matita delle labbra,
al piumino, alla lima: un topo bianco,
d'avorio; e cosí esisti!

2

Ormai nella tua Carinzia
di mirti fioriti e di stagni,
china sul bordo sorvegli
la carpa che timida abbocca
o segui sui tigli, tra gl'irti
pinnacoli le accensioni
del vespro e nell'acque un avvampo
di tende da scali e pensioni.

La sera che si protende
sull'umida conca non porta
col palpito dei motori
che gemiti d'oche e un interno
di nivee maioliche dice
allo specchio annerito che ti vide
diversa una storia di errori
imperturbati e la incide
dove la spugna non giunge.

whirling invisibly
and its calms are even rarer.
I don't know how you manage,
exhausted, in your
heart's great lake of indifference;
maybe some charm protects you,
one you keep near your lipstick,
powder-puff, nail-file: a white mouse
carved in ivory; and so you survive!

2
Now in your own Carinthia
of flowering myrtles and ponds,
you lean at the brink to watch
the shy carp gaping,
or follow beneath the limetrees
the slow kindling of evening
among their ragged peaks
and, down in the water,
a blaze of awnings from the quays and houses.

The evening, extended
over the humid inlet
brings, with the buzzing of motors,
only the cries of geese,
and the snow-white porcelain
interior, tells in the blackened
mirror, that sees you changed,
a story of cool mistakes
etching it in with acid
where the sponge can't reach.

La tua leggenda, Dora!
Ma è scritta già in quegli sguardi
di uomini che hanno fedine
altere e deboli in grandi
ritratti d'oro e ritorna
ad ogni accordo che esprime
l'armonica guasta nell'ora
che abbuia, sempre piú tardi.

E scritta là. Il sempreverde
alloro per la cucina
resiste, la voce non muta,
Ravenna è lontana, distilla
veleno una fede feroce.
Che vuole da te? Non si cede
voce, leggenda o destino...
Ma è tardi, sempre piú tardi.

Lo sai: debbo riperderti e non posso.
Come un tiro aggiustato mi sommuove

Your legend, Dora!
But it is written already
in the looks of those men
with high, weak whiskers
in the big, gold portraits;
it returns in each chord
the cracked harmonica utters
at the far edge of twilight,
later and later.

It's written there. The evergreen
laurel survives for the kitchen,
the voice hasn't changed,
Ravenna's a long way off,
a fierce faith distils poison.
What does it want of you?
Nobody has to surrender
voice, legend, or destiny.
But it is late, it's always
later and later.

                    [D. P. Y.]

THE PLEDGE
Motet I

You know it: I should renounce you and I
    cannot.
With trigger-sureness, everything
    confounds me:

ogni opera, ogni grido e anche lo spiro
salino che straripa
dai moli e fa l'oscura primavera
di Sottoripa.

Paese di ferrame e alberature
a selva nella polvere del vespro.
Un ronzío lungo viene dall'aperto,
strazia com'unghia ai vetri. Cerco il segno
smarrito, il pegno solo ch'ebbi in grazia
da te.
   E l'inferno è certo.

Lontano, ero con te quando tuo padre
entrò nell'ombra e ti lasciò il suo addio.
Che seppi fino allora? Il logorío
di *prima* mi salvò solo per questo:

che t'ignoravo e non dovevo: ai colpi
d'oggi lo so, se di laggiú s'inflette
un'ora e mi riporta Cumerlotti
o Anghébeni – tra scoppi di spolette
e i lamenti e l'accorrer delle squadre.

Each action, every cry, and even
From the piers the salty breath that,
Overflowing, makes the somber springtime
Of Sottoripa.

Region of iron, region of masts that stand
A forest in the dust of evening.
From the open spaces a protracted buzzing
Rasps like a nail upon the windowpane.
   I seek
The lost and only sign, the pledge,
   redemptive, that I had
From you.
          And hell is certain.

               [M. E.]

Motet IV

Long ago, I was with you when your father
died, leaving you only his farewell. That long
wearing away saved me only for this:

I ignored you and shouldn't have: from
   today's
blows I know; if from down there one hour
bends and brings me back Cumerlotti
or Anghebeni — among explosions of fuses
and wails and the scattering of the squads.

               [C. W.]

Addii, fischi nel buio, cenni, tosse
e sportelli abbassati. È l'ora. Forse
gli automi hanno ragione. Come appaiono
dai corridoi, murati!

...

– Presti anche tu alla fioca
litania del tuo rapido quest'orrida
e fedele cadenza di carioca? –

La speranza di pure rivederti
m'abbandonava;

e mi chiesi se questo che mi chiude
ogni senso di te, schermo d'immagini,
ha i segni della morte o dal passato
è in esso, ma distorto e fatto labile,
un *tuo* barbaglio:

(a Modena, tra i portici,
un servo gallonato trascinava
due sciacalli al guinzaglio).

Motet V

Good-byes, whistles in the dark, gestures,
    coughing
and lowered windows. It's time. Maybe
the robots are right. How they loom
from the corridors, walled in!

— Do you, too, lend to the faint litany
of the trains this grotesque
and faithful carioca?

[C. W.]

THE JACKALS AT MODENA
Motet VI

The hope that somehow I might see you again
Was slipping from me;

And I asked myself if what shut me out
From any sense of you — that screen of images —
Bore death's stigmata; or if something of the past
Still lingered in it, but distorted and
    grown tenuous,
Some dazzle of you:

            (At Modena, between the porticoes,
            Came a liveried servant, dragging
            Two jackals on a leash).

[M. E.]

Il saliscendi bianco e nero dei
balestrucci dal palo
del telegrafo al mare
non conforta i tuoi crucci su lo scalo
né ti riporta dove piú non sei.

Già profuma il sambuco fitto su
lo sterrato; il piovasco si dilegua.
Se il chiarore è una tregua,
la tua cara minaccia la consuma.

Ecco il segno; s'innerva
sul muro che s'indora:
un frastaglio di palma
bruciato dai barbagli dell'aurora.

Il passo che proviene
dalla serra sí lieve,
non è felpato dalla neve, è ancora
tua vita, sangue tuo nelle mie vene.

The black and white line
of swallows that rises and falls from the
    telegraph
pole to the sea
doesn't console you, standing at the
    water's edge,
nor take you back to where you no longer are.

Already the elder-tree perfumes, thick
over the excavation; the squall fades away.
If this new brightness is a truce,
your soft threat consumes it.

                                    [C. W.]

BEHOLD THE SIGN
Motet VIII

A sudden pattern struck upon
the wall that glows in gold: behold the sign
edged by the dazzle of the dawn,
the palm's design.

The step that so lightly
comes by the valley lanes,
not sandalled in the snow, is ever
your life, your blood within my veins.

                                    [M. E.]

Perché tardi? Nel pino lo scoiattolo
batte la coda a torcia sulla scorza.
La mezzaluna scende col suo picco
nel sole che la smorza. È giorno fatto.

A un soffio il pigro fumo trasalisce,
si difende nel punto che ti chiude.
Nulla finisce, o tutto, se tu fólgore
lasci la nube.

L'anima che dispensa
furlana e rigodone ad ogni nuova
stagione della strada, s'alimenta
della chiusa passione, la ritrova
a ogni angolo piú intensa.

La tua voce è quest'anima diffusa.
Su fili, su ali, al vento, a caso, col
favore della musa o d'un ordegno,
ritorna lieta o triste. Parlo d'altro,
ad altri che t'ignora e il suo disegno
è là che insiste *do re la sol sol...*

THUNDERBOLT
Motet X

Why do you linger? In the pinetree the squirrel
lashes the flare of his tail along the bark.
The halfmoon slithers with its horn
toward the guttering sun. The day darkens.

At a breath, the lazy smoke swings over
and hovering, overcasts and covers us.
Nothing will end, or everything,
    thunderbolt, if you
out of your cloud start.

                              [M. E.]

Motet XI

The soul that scatters
polka and rigadoon at each
new season of the street, feeds
upon secret passion, finds it fresh
at every turning, more intense.

Your voice is this pervasive soul.
On wires, on wings, in the wind, by chance,
begotten by the muse or some machine,
it comes back gay or sad. I talk of other things
with others, strangers to you; its scheme
is there, insisting do re la sol sol. . .

                              [I. B.]

Infuria sale o grandine? Fa strage
di campanule, svelle la cedrina.
Un rintocco subacqueo s'avvicina,
quale tu lo destavi, e s'allontana.

La pianola degl'inferi da sé
accelera i registri, sale nelle
sfere del gelo... – brilla come te
quando fingevi col tuo trillo d'aria
Lakmé nell'Aria delle Campanelle.

Al primo chiaro, quando
subitaneo un rumore
di ferrovia mi parla
di chiusi uomini in corsa
nel traforo del sasso
illuminato a tagli
da cieli ed acque misti;

al primo buio, quando
il bulino che tarla
la scrivanía rafforza
il suo fervore e il passo
del guardiano s'accosta:

Motet XIV

Is it salt or hail that rages? It lacerates
the campanula, roots out the cedrina.
An underwater tolling comes in waves,
which you awakened, and fades away.

The hurdy-gurdy of the damned
increases tempo, rises
in the spheres of ice. . . − it glitters like you
when, pretending Lakmé, you sang the
   'Bell Song.'
            [C. W.]

Motet XV

At first light, when
the unexpected noise
of a train tells me
of men, enclosed, and carried
through the mountain's tunnel,
illuminated in slices
of mixed sky and water;

at first dark, when
the burin tunneling
in the desk redoubles
its passion, and the footsteps
of the watchman draw near:

al chiaro e al buio, soste ancora umane
se tu a intrecciarle col tuo refe insisti.

Il fiore che ripete
dall'orlo del burrato
non scordarti di me,
non ha tinte piú liete né piú chiare
dello spazio gettato tra me e te.

Un cigolío si sferra, ci discosta,
l'azzurro pervicace non ricompare.
Nell'afa quasi visibile mi riporta all'opposta
tappa, già buia, la funicolare.

La rana, prima a ritentar la corda
dallo stagno che affossa
giunchi e nubi, stormire dei carrubi
conserti dove spenge le sue fiaccole

at dawn and at dusk, pauses still human
if you insist on interweaving them with
    your fierce thread.

                [C. W.]

Motet XVI

The flower that repeats
from the edge of the crevasse
forget me not,
has no tints fairer or more blithe
than the space tossed here between you
    and me.

A clank of metal gears puts us apart.
The stubborn azure fades. In a pall of air
grown almost visible, the funicular
carries me to the opposite stage. The
    dark is there.

           [I. B.]

Motet XVII

The frog, first to sound his chord
from the pond which drowns
rushes and mist; rustle of the woven
carob trees where a sun without heat

un sole senza caldo, tardo ai fiori
ronzío di coleotteri che suggono
ancora linfe, ultimi suoni, avara
vita della campagna. Con un soffio
l'ora s'estingue: un cielo di lavagna
si prepara a un irrompere di scarni
cavalli, alle scintille degli zoccoli.

Non recidere, forbice, quel volto,
solo nella memoria che si sfolla,
non far del grande suo viso in ascolto
la mia nebbia di sempre.

Un freddo cala... Duro il colpo svetta.
E l'acacia ferita da sé scrolla
il guscio di cicala
nella prima belletta di Novembre.

La canna che dispiuma
mollemente il suo rosso
flabello a primavera;

quenches its torches; slow, dragging hum
of coleopters at the flowers,
still sucking blood; last sounds;
avaricious life of the country. With a breath
the hour is extinguished: a slate sky
prepares for the break through of lean
horses, for the sparks of their hooves.

[C. W.]

Motet XVIII

Don't cut, scissors, that face
which remains alone in my emptied memory;
don't make her clear, watchful face
into an unending mist.

A chill descends. . . hard is the cutting blow.
And the wounded mimosa shakes off
the cicada hulls
into the first mud of November.

[C. W.]

Motet XIX

The reed that lightly molts
its soft red crescent
in spring;

la rédola nel fosso, su la nera
correntía sorvolata di libellule;
e il cane trafelato che rincasa
col suo fardello in bocca,

oggi qui non mi tocca riconoscere;
ma là dove il riverbero piú cuoce
e il nuvolo s'abbassa, oltre le sue
pupille ormai remote, solo due
fasci di luce in croce.
                              E il tempo passa.

...ma cosí sia. Un suono di cornetta
dialoga con gli sciami del querceto.
Nella valva che il vespero riflette
un vulcano dipinto fuma lieto.

La moneta incassata nella lava
brilla anch'essa sul tavolo e trattiene
pochi fogli. La vita che sembrava
vasta è piú breve del tuo fazzoletto.

the ditch path in a black current,
overflown by dragon flies;
and the panting dog who comes home,
his burden between his teeth;

today, here, I recognize nothing;
but there, where the light burns hottest
and the cloud descends, beyond your
now-distant pupils, only two
crossed bundles of light.

And time passes.

[C. W.]

LIFE, WHICH HAD SEEMED SO VAST
Motet XX

. . . Well, be it so. The sounding of the horn
answers the bee-swarm in the grove of oaks.
On the seashell which takes the evening's
   gleam
a painted volcano gaily smokes.

In the lava paperweight, a coin, stuck fast,
gleams also on the table, and holds down
   a sheaf
of papers. Life, which had seemed so vast,
is a tinier thing than your handkerchief.

[M. E.]

TEMPI DI BELLOSGUARDO

Oh come là nella corusca
distesa che s'inarca verso i colli,
il brusío della sera s'assottiglia
e gli alberi discorrono col trito
mormorio della rena; come limpida
s'inalvea là in decoro
di colonne e di salci ai lati e grandi salti
di lupi nei giardini, tra le vasche ricolme
che traboccano,
questa vita di tutti non piú posseduta
del nostro respiro;
e come si ricrea una luce di zàffiro
per gli uomini
che vivono laggiú: è troppo triste
che tanta pace illumini a spiragli
e tutto ruoti poi con rari guizzi
su l'anse vaporanti, con incroci
di camini, con grida dai giardini
pensili, con sgomenti e lunghe risa
sui tetti ritagliati, tra le quinte
dei frondami ammassati ed una coda
fulgida che trascorra in cielo prima
che il desiderio trovi le parole!

TIMES AT BELLOSGUARDO

O how faint in the glowing stretch there
that arches towards the hills,
the hubbub of evening grows,
and the trees converse with the petty
murmuring of the sandbanks; how clear
this life finds its channel there
in fine setting of columns, flanked by
    willows and great
leapings of wolves in gardens, between the
    fonts brimming
to overrun,
this life of everyone no longer possesed
by our breath;
and how a sapphire light is born again
for the men
who live down there: it is too sad
that such peace should lighten by glints,
and everything turn then with rare flashes
on the steaming bends, with crossings
of chimneys, with shouts from terraced
gardens, with shakings of the heart and
    laughing, long,
on the roofs, sharp-traced, between
    the wings
of massed branching and a trailing end,
luminous, which passes to heaven, before
desire finds the words!
. . .

Derelitte sul poggio
fronde della magnolia
verdibrune se il vento
porta dai frigidari
dei pianterreni un travolto
concitamento d'accordi
ed ogni foglia che oscilla
o rilampeggia nel folto
in ogni fibra s'imbeve
di quel saluto, e piú ancora
derelitte le fronde
dei vivi che si smarriscono
nel prisma del minuto,
le membra di febbre votate
al moto che si ripete
in circolo breve: sudore
che pulsa, sudore di morte,
atti minuti specchiati,
sempre gli stessi, rifranti
echi del batter che in alto
sfaccetta il sole e la pioggia,
fugace altalena tra vita
che passa e vita che sta,
quassú non c'è scampo: si muore
sapendo o si sceglie la vita
che muta ed ignora: altra morte.
E scende la cuna tra logge

Desolate on the rise,
foliage of the magnolia
green-brown if the wind
carries from icy rooms
of ground floors a distorted
excitement of harmony
and every leaf that shakes
or twinkles in the bush
drinks at every fibre
that greeting, and still more
desolate the foliage
of the living who are lost
in the prism of the minute,
the feverish limbs devoted
to the motion that recurs
in a brief circle: sweat
that throbs, sweat of death,
acts minutes mirrored,
always the same, refracted
echoes of the striking which on high
cuts facets in the sun and rain,
fugitive swing between life
that passes and life that stays,
up here there is no escape: we die
knowingly or choose the life
that changes and does not know: another
    death.
And the cradle goes down between the
    galleries

ed erme: l'accordo commuove
le lapidi che hanno veduto
le immagini grandi, l'onore,
l'amore inflessibile, il giuoco,
la fedeltà che non muta.
E il gesto rimane: misura
il vuoto, ne sonda il confine:
il gesto ignoto che esprime
sé stesso e non altro: passione
di sempre in un sangue e un cervello
irripetuti; e fors'entra
nel chiuso e lo forza con l'esile
sua punta di grimaldello.

LA CASA DEI DOGANIERI

Tu non ricordi la casa dei doganieri
sul rialzo a strapiombo sulla scogliera:
desolata t'attende dalla sera
in cui v'entrò lo sciame dei tuoi pensieri
e vi sostò irrequieto.

Libeccio sferza da anni le vecchie mura
e il suono del tuo riso non è piú lieto:

and the pillared busts: the harmony affects
the stones that have seen
the great images, honour,
unbending love, the game of chance,
faith which does not alter.
And the gesture lingers: measures
the void, sounds out its boundaries:
the unknown gesture which expresses
itself and nothing else: passion
of all time in blood and a brain
not to be repeated; and perhaps it enters
the closed place and forces it with its fine
point like a picklock's.

                              [G. K.]

THE SHOREWATCHERS' HOUSE

You don't remember the shorewatchers' house
above the rock-reef, sheer, upon the height:
it waits for you bereavedly since the night
the swarm of your thoughts came there
    to house,
unquietly to stay.

South-westers have thrashed the old
    walls for years
and your laughter's ring is no longer gay:

73

la bussola va impazzita all'avventura
e il calcolo dei dadi piú non torna.
Tu non ricordi; altro tempo frastorna
la tua memoria; un filo s'addipana.

Ne tengo ancora un capo; ma s'allontana
la casa e in cima al tetto la banderuola
affumicata gira senza pietà.
Ne tengo un capo; ma tu resti sola
né qui respiri nell'oscurità.

Oh l'orizzonte in fuga, dove s'accende
rara la luce della petroliera!
Il varco è qui? (Ripullula il frangente
ancora sulla balza che scoscende...)
Tu non ricordi la casa di questa
mia sera. Ed io non so chi va e chi resta.

EASTBOURNE

'Dio salvi il Re' intonano le trombe
da un padiglione erto su palafitte
che aprono il varco al mare quando sale

the compass, at hazard, crazily veers
and the dice no longer favour our bets.
You don't remember; another time besets
your memory; and a thread is wound.

I still hold an end of it; but the distant-bound
house keeps receding, the blackened
    weathervane,
spinning on the roof-top pitiless, stark.
I hold an end of it; but you remain
alone nor breathe here in the dark.

O the skyline in retreat where, flaring,
the tanker's light shows rarely on the verge!
Is this the crossing-point? (The breakers seethe
even now at cliffs which crash with every
    surge. . .)
You don't remember the house of this my
    evening.
And I don't know who stays and who is
    leaving.
                [G. K.]

EASTBOURNE

"God Save the King" the trumpets
    moan and groan
From a pavilion high on piles
That gape to let the sea through when it comes

a distruggere peste
umide di cavalli nella sabbia
del litorale.

Freddo un vento m'investe
ma un guizzo accende i vetri
e il candore di mica delle rupi
ne risplende.

Bank Holiday... Riporta l'onda lunga
della mia vita
a striscio, troppo dolce sulla china.
Si fa tardi. I fragori si distendono,
si chiudono in sordina.

Vanno su sedie a ruote i mutilati,
li accompagnano cani dagli orecchi
lunghi, bimbi in silenzio o vecchi. (Forse
domani tutto parrà un sogno.)
                                E vieni
tu pure voce prigioniera, sciolta
anima ch'è smarrita,
voce di sangue, persa e restituita
alla mia sera.

Come lucente muove sui suoi spicchi
la porta di un albergo
– risponde un'altra e le rivolge un raggio –

To wash out wet
Horse-hoofmarks on the sand
Of this sea-shore.

Coldly the wind claws me
But a burning light snakes along the windows
And white mica of cliffs
Glitters in that glare.

Bank Holiday. . . . It brings back the
    long wave
Of my own life,
Creeping and sliding, sluggish up the slope.
It's getting late. The brassy noise balloons
And sags to silence.

There come now on their wheel-chairs the
    cripples.
There accompany them dogs with long
Ears, silent children, and old folk. (Possibly
Tomorrow it will all seem a dream).

                        And you come,
You, pure voice, long imprisoned, spirit now
Set free but with no bearings yet,
The blood's voice, lost and given back
To the evening of my days.

As a hotel's revolving door
Moves shiningly upon its four leaves –
One leaf answers another, flashing a message! –

m'agita un carosello che travolge
tutto dentro il suo giro; ed io in ascolto
('mia patria!') riconosco il tuo respiro,
anch'io mi levo e il giorno è troppo folto.

Tutto apparirà vano: anche la forza
che nella sua tenace ganga aggrega
i vivi e i morti, gli alberi e gli scogli
e si svolge da te, per te. La festa
non ha pietà. Rimanda
il suo scroscio la banda, si dispiega
nel primo buio una bontà senz'armi.

Vince il male... La ruota non s'arresta.

Anche tu lo sapevi, luce-in-tenebra.

Nella plaga che brucia, dove sei
scomparsa al primo tocco delle campane, solo
rimane l'acre tizzo che già fu
Bank Holiday.

BARCHE SULLA MARNA

Felicità del súghero abbandonato
alla corrente
che stempra attorno i ponti rovesciati

So I am moved by a merry-go-round that
   sweeps
Everything up in its whirl; alertly listening
("My country!") I recognise your breathing,
And get up; it grows too stuffy, this day.

Everything will seem pointless: even the strength
That in its gritty matrix aggregates
Living and dead, trees and rocks,
And from you, through you, unfolds. Holidays
Have no pity. The band expands
Its blare of sound, in the first dusk
An unarmed goodness spreads itself around.

Evil conquers. . . The wheel does not stop:

Also Thou knewest this, Lux-in-Tenebris!

In this burnt quarter of sky, whence at the first
Clang of bells Thou departedst, only
The guttering torch remains that, already, *was*
And is not, *Bank Holiday.*

               [G. S. F.]

BOATS ON THE MARNE

The bliss of cork yielding
to the current
that stipples around the overturned bridges

e il plenilunio pallido nel sole:
barche sul fiume, agili nell'estate
e un murmure stagnante di città.
Segui coi remi il prato se il cacciatore
di farfalle vi giunge con la sua rete,
l'alberaia sul muro dove il sangue
del drago si ripete nel cinabro.

Voci sul fiume, scoppi dalle rive,
o ritmico scandire di piroghe
nel vespero che cola
tra le chiome dei noci, ma dov'è
la lenta processione di stagioni
che fu un'alba infinita e senza strade,
dov'è la lunga attesa e qual è il nome
del vuoto che ci invade.

Il sogno è questo: un vasto,
interminato giorno che rifonde
tra gli argini, quasi immobile, il suo bagliore
e ad ogni svolta il buon lavoro dell'uomo,
il domani velato che non fa orrore.
E altro ancora era il sogno, ma il suo riflesso
fermo sull'acqua in fuga, sotto il nido
del pendolino, aereo e inaccessibile,
era silenzio altissimo nel grido
concorde del meriggio ed un mattino
piú lungo era la sera, il gran fermento
era grande riposo.

and the fullblown moon ghostly in sunlight:
nimble boats on the river, it's summer,
the sluggish drone of the city.
With oarstrokes you follow the field if the
butterfly catcher's net will reach it,
and the thicket topping the wall where
dragon's-blood repeats in the cinnabar.

A river of voices, bankside explosions,
or rhythmic scansion of canoes
in the halflight sieved through the shag
of the walnut trees; but where is
the easy procession of seasons
which was an infinite dawn without roads —
where is the long expectation and what is
the name of the void that invades us.

This is the dream: a vast
unending day that nearly motionless
recasts its splendor between the banks,
and men's good works at every turn,
a veiled tomorrow that holds no terror.
And the dream was something more,
    but its echo
fixed on the fleeing waters under
the penduline's nest, airy and aloof,
sank like silence in the afternoon's
concert of cries and evening was a longer
morning, the great commotion
great rest.

Qui... il colore
che resiste è del topo che ha saltato
tra i giunchi o col suo spruzzo di metallo
velenoso, lo storno che sparisce
tra i fumi della riva.
                    Un altro giorno,
ripeti – o che ripeti? E dove porta
questa bocca che brúlica in un getto
solo?
            La sera è questa. Ora possiamo
scendere fino a che s'accenda l'Orsa.

(Barche sulla Marna, domenicali, in corsa
nel dí della tua festa.)

NOTIZIE DALL'AMIATA

Il fuoco d'artifizio del maltempo
sarà murmure d'arnie a tarda sera.
La stanza ha travature
tarlate ed un sentore di meloni
penetra dall'assito. Le fumate
morbide che risalgono una valle
d'elfi e di funghi fino al cono diafano
della cima m'intorbidano i vetri,

Here. . . is the enduring color
of the rat that jumped
through the rushes or the starling's spurt of
poison-green metal vanishing
in the mists on shore.
                        Another day done,
you repeat — or what were you saying?
   And where
does this outlet lead swarming in a single
gush?
      Evening is like this. Now we can drift
   downstream
till the Great Bear kindles.

(Boats on the Marne in Sunday races,
your birthday.)
                        [S. R. and A. de P.]

NEWS FROM AMIATA

The fireworks of threatening weather
might be murmur of hives at duskfall.
The room has pockmarked beams
and an odor of melons
seeps from the store-room. Soft mists
that climb from a valley
of elves and mushrooms to the diaphanous
   cone
of the crest cloud over my windows

e ti scrivo di qui, da questo tavolo
remoto, dalla cellula di miele
di una sfera lanciata nello spazio –
e le gabbie coperte, il focolare
dove i marroni esplodono, le vene
di salnitro e di muffa sono il quadro
dove tra poco romperai. La vita
che t'affàbula è ancora troppo breve
se ti contiene! Schiude la tua icona
il fondo luminoso. Fuori piove.

. . .

E tu seguissi le fragili architetture
annerite dal tempo e dal carbone,
i cortili quadrati che hanno nel mezzo
il pozzo profondissimo; tu seguissi
il volo infagottato degli uccelli
notturni e in fondo al borro l'allucciolío
della Galassia, la fascia d'ogni tormento.
Ma il passo che risuona a lungo nell'oscuro
è di chi va solitario e altro non vede
che questo cadere di archi, di ombre e di pieghe.
Le stelle hanno trapunti troppo sottili,
l'occhio del campanile è fermo sulle due ore,
i rampicanti anch'essi sono un'ascesa
di tenebre ed il loro profumo duole amaro.
Ritorna domani piú freddo, vento del nord,
spezza le antiche mani dell'arenaria,
sconvolgi i libri d'ore nei solai,

and I write you from here, from this table,
remote, from the honey cell
of a sphere launched into space −
and the covered cages, the hearth
where chestnuts are bursting, the veins
of saltpetre and mould, are the frame
where soon you will break through.
Life that enfables you is still too brief
if it contains you. The luminous ground
unfolds your icon. Outside it rains.

. . .

Could you but see the fragile buildings
blackened by time and smoke,
the square courtyards with their deep wells
at center; and could you see
the laden flight of the night birds
and, beyond the ravine, the twinkling
of the Galaxy that soothes all wounds!
But the step that echoes long in the dark
is of one who goes alone and who sees only
this fall of shadows, of arches and of folds.
The stars sew with too fine a thread,
the eye of the tower stopped at two,
even the climbing vines are an ascent
    of shadows,
and their perfume bitter hurt.
Return tomorrow, colder, wind from the north,
shatter the old hands of the sandstone,
overturn the books of hours in the sunrooms,

e tutto sia lente tranquilla, dominio, prigione
del senso che non dispera! Ritorna piú forte
vento di settentrione che rendi care
le catene e suggelli le spore del possibile!

Son troppo strette le strade, gli asini neri
che zoccolano in fila dànno scintille,
dal picco nascosto rispondono vampate di magnesio.
Oh il gocciolío che scende a rilento
dalle casipole buie, il tempo fatto acqua,
il lungo colloquio coi poveri morti, la cenere,
                                                    il vento,
il vento che tarda, la morte, la morte che vive!
 . . .
Questa rissa cristiana che non ha
se non parole d'ombra e di lamento
che ti porta di me? Meno di quanto
t'ha rapito la gora che s'interra
dolce nella sua chiusa di cemento.
Una ruota di mola, un vecchio tronco,
confini ultimi al mondo. Si disfà
un cumulo di strame: e tardi usciti
a unire la mia veglia al tuo profondo
sonno che li riceve, i porcospini
s'abbeverano a un filo di pietà.

and let all be pendulum calm, dominion,
    prison of sense
which does not know despair! Return still
    stronger
wind from the north, wind that endears
our chains and seals the spores of the possible!
The paths are too narrow, the hooves of the
    black donkeys
clicking in file raise sparks,
from the hidden peak magnesium flares reply.
O the slow drip of rain from the dark shacks,
time turned to water,
the long colloquy with the poor dead,
    the ashes, the wind,
late-coming wind, and death, and death
    that lives!

. . .

This christian fracas which has no speech
other than shadows or laments,
what does it give you of me? Less
than was snatched from you by the tunnel
plunging gently into its casing of stone.
A mill-wheel, an old tree-trunk,
last boundaries of the world. A heap
of chaff blows off; and, venturing late,
to join my vigil to your deep sleep
that welcomes them, the porcupines
will sip at a thin stream of pity.
                                    [I. B.]

NEWS FROM MOUNT AMIATA

I
Come night,
the ugly weather's fire-cracker simmer
will deepen to the gruff buzz of beehives.
Termites tunnel the public room's rafters
    to sawdust,
an odor of bruised melons oozes from the
    floor.
A sick smoke lifts from the elf-huts and
    funghi of the valley —
like an eagle climbs our mountain's bald cone,
and soils the windows.
I drag my table to the window,
and write to you —
here on this mountain, in this beehive cell
on the globe rocketed through space.
My letter is a paper hoop.
When I break through it, you will be
    imprisoned.

Here mildew sprouts like grass from
    the floor,
the canary cage is hooded with dirty
    green serge,
chestnuts explode on the grate.
Outside, it's raining.
There you are legendary.
Any legend falls short, if it confine you,
your gold-gated icon unfolding on gold.

2

Magnesium flares light up the hidden
    summits;
but the narrow feudal streets below are too
    dark
for the caravan of black donkeys kicking
    up sparks.

You are devoted to precarious
sentiments and sediment − blackened
    architecture;
rectangular courtyards centered
on bottomless wells. You are led
by the sinister wings of nightbirds,
the infinite pit, the luminous gape of the
    galaxies −
all their sleight of hand and torture.
But the step that carries out into darkness
comes from the man going alone,
who sees nothing but the nearest
    light-chinked shutter.
The stars' pattern is too deep for him,
atmospheric ivy only chokes his darkness,
his campanile shuts its eye at two o'clock.

3

Here on this mountain,
the world has no custom-barriers.
Let tomorrow be colder, let the north wind
shatter the stringy ribbons of old Missals,
the sandstone bastion of the barbarians.

When our sensations have no self-assurance,
everything must be a lens.
Then the polar winds will return clearer,
and convert us to our chains, the chains
    of the possible.

4
Today, the monotonous oratory of the dead,
ashes, lethargic winds —
a reluctant trickle drips
from the thatched huts.
Time is water.
The rain rains down black letters —
a *contemptu mundi!* What part of me does
    it bring you?

Now at this late hour
of my watch and your endless, prodigal sleep,
my tiny straw city is breaking up.
The porcupine sips a quill of mercy.

                                [R. L.]

LA BUFERA E ALTRO

THE STORM AND OTHER THINGS

LA BUFERA

Les princes n'ont point d'yeux pour voir ces grand's merveilles,
Leurs mains ne servent plus qu'à nous persécuter...

(Agrippa D'Aubigné: À Dieu.)

La bufera che sgronda sulle foglie
dure della magnolia i lunghi tuoni
marzolini e la grandine,

(i suoni di cristallo nel tuo nido
notturno ti sorprendono, dell'oro
che s'è spento sui mogani, sul taglio
dei libri rilegati, brucia ancora
una grana di zucchero nel guscio
delle tue palpebre)

il lampo che candisce
alberi e muri e li sorprende in quella
eternità d'istante – marmo manna
e distruzione – ch'entro te scolpita
porti per tua condanna e che ti lega
piú che l'amore a me, strana sorella, –
e poi lo schianto rude, i sistri, il fremere
dei tamburelli sulla fossa fuia,
lo scalpicciare del fandango, e sopra
qualche gesto che annaspa...

Come quando
ti rivolgesti e con la mano, sgombra
la fronte dalla nube dei capelli,

mi salutasti – per entrar nel buio.

THE STORM

Les princes n'ont point d'yeux pour voir ces grands merveilles,
Leurs mains ne servent plus qu'à nous persécuter . . .
Agrippa D'Aubigné: "A Dieu"

The storm that pelts the tough leaves
of the magnolia with long
March thunders, with hailstones,

(crystal sounds in your nighttime
nest startle you; what's left of the gold
doused on the mahogany, on the tooling
of bound books, still burns
a grain of sugar in the shell
of your eyelids)

the lightning blaze that candies
trees and walls surprising them in this
forever of an instant — marble, manna
and destruction — which you bear carved
inside you, your condemnation, and lashes
you to me, strange sister, more than love —
and then the rough crash, rattles, thrill of
timbrels over the hidden pit,
the stamp of the fandango, and beyond it
some groping gesture. . .

The way it was when
you turned, your forehead brushed
of a cloud of hair,

and waved to me — and stepped into darkness.

[S. R. and A. de P.]

LUNGOMARE

Il soffio cresce, il buio è rotto a squarci,
e l'ombra che tu mandi sulla fragile
palizzata s'arriccia. Troppo tardi

se vuoi esser te stessa! Dalla palma
tonfa il sorcio, il baleno è sulla miccia,
sui lunghissimi cigli del tuo sguardo.

SU UNA LETTERA NON SCRITTA

Per un formicolío d'albe, per pochi
fili su cui s'impigli
il fiocco della vita e s'incollani
in ore e in anni, oggi i delfini a coppie
capriolano coi figli? Oh ch'io non oda
nulla di te, ch'io fugga dal bagliore
dei tuoi cigli. Ben altro è sulla terra.

Sparir non so né riaffacciarmi; tarda
la fucina vermiglia
della notte, la sera si fa lunga,
la preghiera è supplizio e non ancora
tra le rocce che sorgono t'è giunta
la bottiglia. dal mare. L'onda, vuota,
si rompe sulla punta, a Finisterre.

LUNGOMARE

The puff increases, the dark is torn to shreds,
and the shadow you transmit to the frail
palisade bristles. Too too late

if you want to be yourself! From the palm
plops the mouse, lightning's at the wick,
on the longest lashes of your look.

                                    [C. C.]

A LETTER NOT WRITTEN

Is it for tingling daybreaks, for a few
threads on which the tassel of
life snags and is strung into hours
and years, that paired dolphins are
sporting today with their young? Oh to hear
nothing of you, to escape the dazzle
of your look. There's more than this on earth.

I cannot vanish nor reappear; night's
vermilion forge starts late,
the evening drags on;
prayer is torture and not yet among
the towering rocks has the bottle
reached you from the sea. The empty
breaker shatters on the point at Finisterre.

                           [S. R. and A. de P.]

NEL SONNO

Il canto delle strigi, quando un'iride
con intermessi palpiti si stinge,
i gemiti e i sospiri
di gioventú, l'errore che recinge
le tempie e il vago orror dei cedri smossi
dall'urto della notte – tutto questo
può ritornarmi, traboccar dai fossi,
rompere dai condotti, farmi desto
alla tua voce. Punge il suono d'una
giga crudele, l'avversario chiude
la celata sul viso. Entra la luna
d'amaranto nei chiusi occhi, è una nube
che gonfia; e quando il sonno la trasporta
piú in fondo, è ancora sangue oltre la morte.

LA FRANGIA DEI CAPELLI...

La frangia dei capelli che ti vela
la fronte puerile, tu distrarla

IN SLEEP

The cries of screech-owls, or the intermittent
    heartbeats
of dying butterflies,
or the tossing and turning
sighs of the young, or the bald error that
    tightens
like a garrote around the temples, or the
    vague horror
of upturned cedars in the onrush of sleep —
    all this
can come back to me, overflowing from ditches,
bursting from waterpipes, and make me
    wide awake
to your voice. The music of a slow,
    demented dance
cuts through; the enemy clangs down
his visor, hiding his face. The amaranth moon
enters behind the closed eyelids,
    becomes a swelling
cloud; and when sleep takes it
deeper in, it is still blood beyond any death.
                                    [C. W.]

THE STRANDS OF HAIR...

Don't push back the strands of hair which
    veil
your child-like forehead. They, too, speak

101

con la mano non devi. Anch'essa parla
di te, sulla mia strada è tutto il cielo,
la sola luce con le giade ch'ài
accerchiate sul polso, nel tumulto
del sonno la cortina che gl'indulti
tuoi distendono, l'ala onde tu vai,
trasmigratrice Artemide ed illesa,
tra le guerre dei nati-morti; e s'ora
d'aeree lanugini s'infiora
quel fondo, a marezzarlo sei tu, scesa
d'un balzo, e irrequieta la tua fronte
si confonde con l'alba, la nasconde.

A MIA MADRE

Ora che il coro delle coturnici
ti blandisce nel sonno eterno, rotta
felice schiera in fuga verso i clivi
vendemmiati del Mesco, or che la lotta
dei viventi piú infuria, se tu cedi
come un'ombra la spoglia
           (e non è un'ombra,
o gentile, non è ciò che tu credi)

of you − they are the whole sky wherever
    I go,
my only light except for the jades
which circle your wrist; in the riot
of sleep they drop like curtains, bringing
your amnesties; they carry you,
transmigratory Artemis, unharmed
among the blood-baths of the still-born;
    and, if now
hair light as down flowers
upon that brow, you, come down from
    some height,
alter its color, your restless forehead
covers the dawn, and hides it.

                                        [C. W.]

TO MY MOTHER

Now that the chorus of the rock partridge
lulls you in the eternal sleep and the gay,
broken band is in flight toward the hills
of Mesco, long picked clean of their harvest;
    now that the struggle
of the living rages even stronger,
    if you yield up,
like a shadow, your last remains
                            (and it isn't a shadow,
it isn't kind − it isn't what you think)

chi ti proteggerà? La strada sgombra
non è una via, solo due mani, un volto,
quelle mani, *quel* volto, il gesto d'una
vita che non è un'altra ma se stessa,
solo questo ti pone nell'eliso
folto d'anime e voci in cui tu vivi;

e la domanda che tu lasci è anch'essa
un gesto tuo, all'ombra delle croci.

BALLATA SCRITTA IN UNA CLINICA

Nel solco dell'emergenza:

quando si sciolse oltremonte
la folle cometa agostana
nell'aria ancora serena

– ma buio, per noi, e terrore
e crolli di altane e di ponti
su noi come Giona sepolti
nel ventre della balena –

ed io mi volsi e lo specchio
di me più non era lo stesso

who will protect you? The cleared highway
is not a passage; only two hands, a face,
those hands, *that* face, the gestures of a life
that is nothing but itself –
only this puts you into the heaven
thick with the souls and voices that
    you live by;

and the question you leave unanswered
    is also
only a gesture in the shadow of the crosses.

                                        [C. W.]

BALLAD WRITTEN IN A CLINIC

In the furrow of emergency:

when the lunatic comet of August
was loosed beyond the mountains
in the still serene air

– but darkness, for us, and terror,
bridges and belvederes collapsing
above us, buried deep, like Jonah
in the belly of the whale –

I turned away and the mirror
said I was not the same

perché la gola ed il petto
t'avevano chiuso di colpo
in un manichino di gesso.

Nel cavo delle tue orbite
brillavano lenti di lacrime
piú spesse di questi tuoi grossi
occhiali di tartaruga
che a notte ti tolgo e avvicino
alle fiale della morfina.

L'iddio taurino non era
il nostro, ma il Dio che colora
di fuoco i gigli del fosso:
Ariete invocai e la fuga
del mostro cornuto travolse
con l'ultimo orgoglio anche il cuore
schiantato dalla tua tosse.

Attendo un cenno, se è prossima
l'ora del ratto finale:
son pronto e la penitenza
s'inizia fin d'ora nel cupo
singulto di valli e dirupi
dell'*altra* Emergenza.

Hai messo sul comodino
il bulldog di legno, la sveglia
col fosforo sulle lancette
che spande un tenue lucore
sul tuo dormiveglia,

because the throat and the chest
of a chalk mannequin
had suddenly encased you.

In the deep sockets of your eyes
shone lenses of tears
thicker than your heavy
tortoiseshell glasses
which I remove at night and place
next to the vials of morphine.

The bull-god was not ours, but
the God who ignites
the lilies in the ditch:
I summoned Aries and the horned
beast's passage swept away
the last shreds of pride, even the heart
cracked from your coughing.

I wait for a sign that the hour
of final abduction is near:
I am ready, and penitence
begins then, a hollow
weeping from the peaks and valleys
of the *other* emergency.

On your bureau you kept
the wooden bulldog, the alarm-clock
with the phosphorus hands
which shed a tenuous splendor
on your drowsings, half-awake,

il nulla che basta a chi vuole
forzare la porta stretta;
e fuori, rossa, s'inasta,
si spiega sul bianco una croce.

Con te anch'io m'affaccio alla voce
che irrompe nell'alba, all'enorme
presenza dei morti; e poi l'ululo

del cane di legno è il mio, muto.

DUE NEL CREPUSCOLO

Fluisce fra te e me sul belvedere
un chiarore subacqueo che deforma
col profilo dei colli anche il tuo viso.
Sta in un fondo sfuggevole, reciso
da te ogni gesto tuo; entra senz'orma,
e sparisce, nel mezzo che ricolma
ogni solco e si chiude sul tuo passo:
con me tu qui, dentro quest'aria scesa
a sigillare
il torpore dei massi.

                              Ed io riverso
nel potere che grava attorno, cedo
al sortilegio di non riconoscere

the nothingness — enough for those
who mean to force the narrow gate;
outside now, red on white,
a cross hoists and unfurls.

With you I turn toward the voice
which breaks in the dawn, the enormous
presence of the dead; the soundless howl

of the wooden dog is mine.

[D. P. Y. and V. R.]

TWO IN THE TWILIGHT

Between you and me on the belvedere flows
a subaqueous gleam that distorts
the hills' outline and with it your face.
Against a fleeting background, cut off
from you, stands your each gesture;
   it enters traceless
and disappears, in the medium which annuls
every wake and closes on your step:
with me you, here, within this air
which came down to seal
the lethargy of boulders.
          And I, overwhelmed
by the power impending around, surrender
to the sorcery of no longer recognizing

di me piú nulla fuor di me; s'io levo
appena il braccio, mi si fa diverso
l'atto, si spezza su un cristallo, ignota
e impallidita sua memoria, e il gesto
già piú non m'appartiene;
se parlo, ascolto quella voce attonito,
scendere alla sua gamma piú remota
o spenta all'aria che non la sostiene.

Tale nel punto che resiste all'ultima
consunzione del giorno
dura lo smarrimento; poi un soffio
risolleva le valli in un frenetico
moto e deriva dalle fronde un tinnulo
suono che si disperde
tra rapide fumate e i primi lumi
disegnano gli scali.

     . . . le parole
tra noi leggere cadono. Ti guardo
in un molle riverbero. Non so
se ti conosco; so che mai diviso
fui da te come accade in questo tardo
ritorno. Pochi istanti hanno bruciato
tutto di noi: fuorché due volti, due
maschere che s'incidono, sforzate,
di un sorriso.

anything of me outside me: if merely I lift
my arm, the act
is altered, shattered on a crystal, then
its memory turns strange and faded,
    and the gesture
no longer belongs to me;
if I speak, I listen to that voice astonished,
as it descends to its farthest range
or dies in the unsustaining air.

Such at the point of last resistance
in the death agony of day
the bewilderment lasts; then a gust
raises the valley again in
turmoil and from the fronds elicits a tinkling
sound soon lost
among swift coils of smoke and the first
    lights
outline the piers.
                    . . .words
fall light between us. I look at you
in a soft dusk. I do not know
if I know you; this I know, that never
was I divided from you as in this late
return. A few instants have burned
everything of us: except two faces, two
masks that carve upon themselves
a smile.
        [G. C.]

VISITA A FADIN

Passata la Madonna dell'Orto e seguíti per pochi passi i portici del centro svoltai poi su per la rampa che conduce all'ospedale e giunsi in breve dove il malato non si attendeva di vedermi: sulla balconata degli incurabili, stesi al sole. Mi scorse subito e non parve sorpreso. Aveva sempre i capelli cortissimi, rasi da poco, il viso piú scavato e rosso agli zigomi, gli occhi bellissimi, come prima, ma dissolti in un alone piú profondo. Giungevo senza preavviso, e in giorno indebito: neppure la sua Carlina, "l'angelo musicante", poteva esser là.

Il mare, in basso, era vuoto, e sulla costa apparivano sparse le architetture di marzapane degli arricchiti.

Ultima sosta del viaggio: alcuni dei tuoi compagni occasionali (operai, commessi, parrucchieri) ti avevano già preceduto alla chetichella, sparendo dai loro lettucci. T'eri portato alcuni pacchi di libri, li avevi messi al posto del tuo zaino d'un tempo: vecchi libri fuor di moda, a eccezione di un volumetto di poesie che presi e che ora resterà con me, come indovinammo tutti e due senza dirlo.

Del colloquio non ricordo piú nulla. Certo non aveva bisogno di richiamarsi alle questioni supreme, agli universali, chi era sempre vis-

VISIT TO FADIN

Passed the Madonna dell'Orto and followed for
some steps the colonnade of the center and I
turned then up over the ramp that leads to the
hospital and quickly reached the sick man who
didn't expect to see me: on the balcony for the
incurable, out in the sun. He saw me at once and
didn't seem surprised. He still had the shortest
hair, shaved but a while ago, his face hollower
and redder at the cheekbones, the most beautiful
eyes, as before, but dissolved in a deeper halo. I
arrived without advance notice, and on a wrong
day: not even his Carlina, "the musical angel,"
could be there.

The sea, down below, was empty, and along
the coast the marzipan architecture of the rich
looked skimpy.

The last stop: some of your erstwhile compan-
ions (workers, clerks, hairdressers) had already
preceded you stealthily, vanishing from their
cots. You had brought along some bundles of
books, had set them out by the knapsack you
used to carry: old books out of fashion, with the
exception of one small volume of poetry that I
took and that now will remain with me, as we
both guessed without saying so.

Of our conversation I remember nothing. Cer-
tainly there was no need for him to revert to the
supreme questions, the universals, he who had

suto in modo umano, cioè semplice e silenzioso. Exit Fadin. E ora dire che non ci sei più è dire solo che sei entrato in un ordine diverso, per quanto quello in cui ci muoviamo noi ritardatari, cosí pazzesco com'è, sembri alla nostra ragione l'unico in cui la divinità può svolgere i propri attributi, riconoscersi e saggiarsi nei limiti di un assunto di cui ignoriamo il significato. (Anch'essa, dunque, avrebbe bisogno di noi? Se è una bestemmia, ahimè, non è neppure la nostra peggiore.)
Essere sempre tra i primi e *sapere*, ecco ciò che conta, anche se il perché della rappresentazione ci sfugge. Chi ha avuto da te quest'alta lezione di *decenza quotidiana* (la piú difficile delle virtú) può attendere senza fretta il libro delle tue reliquie. La tua parola non era forse di quelle che si scrivono.

VERSO SIENA

Ohimè che la memoria sulla vetta
non ha chi la trattenga!

(La fuga dei porcelli sull'Ambretta
notturna al sobbalzare della macchina
che guada, il carillon di San Gusmè
e una luna maggenga, tutta macchie...)

always lived as a human being, simply and si-
lently. Exit Fadin. And now to say that you no
longer are is to say only that you have entered
a different order, insofar as that wherein we
move we laggards, as crazy as it is, you seem to
our senses the only one in whom divinity can
reveal her proper attributes, be recognized and be
savored within the limits of an assumption whose
significance we don't know. (Should even she,
then, have need of us? If this is blasphemy, alas,
it's hardly our worst.)

To be always amongst the first and to *know*,
this is what matters, even if the reason for the
performance escapes us. He who had had from
you this high lesson of *quotidian decency* (the
most difficult virtue of all) can await unhurried
the book of your relics. Your word was not per-
haps of those that get written.

[C. C.]

TOWARDS SIENA

Agh, that memory at its fullest
has no one to hold it back!

(The flight of pigs on the night mudflats
of the Ambretta as the car bounces, fords the
    river;
then the carillon of San Gusme;
and a May moon, all stains. . .)

La scatola a sorpresa ha fatto scatto
sul punto in cui il mio Dio gittò la maschera
e fulminò il ribelle.

SULLA GREVE

Ora non ceno solo con lo sguardo
come quando al mio fischio ti sporgevi
e ti vedevo appena. Un masso, un solco
a imbuto, il volo nero d'una rondine,
un coperchio sul mondo...

E m'è pane quel boccio di velluto
che s'apre su un glissato di mandolino,
acqua il frúscio scorrente, il tuo profondo
respiro vino.

DI UN NATALE METROPOLITANO
Londra

Un vischio, fin dall'infanzia sospeso grappolo
di fede e di pruina sul tuo lavandino
e sullo specchio ovale ch'ora adombrano
i tuoi ricci bergère fra santini e ritratti

The jack-in-the-box has sprung open
where my God threw down his mask,
hurled lightning at the rebel.

[C. W.]

SULLA GREVE

Now I sup not only with your look
as when at my whistle you stretched out
and I would hardly see you. A rock, a streak
with a funnel, the swallow's black flight,
a covering for the world. . .

And to me bread is that velvet bud
that opens at a mandolin glissando,
water the flowing rustle, your profound
breath wine.

[C. C.]

A METROPOLITAN CHRISTMAS
London

Mistletoe, from childhood a hanging cluster
of faith and hoar-frost over your washstand
and the oval mirror which your shepherd-
    curls
now shade among the paper saints and
    photographs

di ragazzi infilati un po' alla svelta
nella cornice, una caraffa vuota,
bicchierini di cenere e di bucce,
le luci di Mayfair, poi a un crocicchio
le anime, le bottiglie che non seppero aprirsi,
non piú guerra né pace, il tardo frullo
di un piccione incapace di seguirti
sui gradini automatici che ti slittano in giú...

LASCIANDO UN « DOVE »
Cattedrale di Ely

Una colomba bianca m'ha disceso
fra stele, sotto cuspidi dove il cielo s'annida.
Albe e luci, sospese; ho amato il sole,
il colore del miele, or chiedo il bruno,
chiedo il fuoco che cova, questa tomba
che non vola, il tuo sguardo che la sfida.

ARGYLL TOUR
Glasgow

I bimbi sotto il cedro, funghi o muffe
vivi dopo l'acquata,
il puledrino in gabbia

of boys slipped helter-skelter into
the frame; an empty decanter,
small glasses of ashes and rinds,
the lights of Mayfair; later, souls at a crossing,
bottles which could not open themselves –
no longer war or peace; the final whirr
of a pigeon unable to follow you
on the escalator which slides you down. . .

[C. W.]

LEAVING A 'DOVE'
Ely Cathedral

A white dove has lowered me
among stelae, under spires where the sky nests.
Dawns and lights, suspended; I have loved
   the sun,
the color of honey; now I ask for the dark,
I ask for the fire that smolders, this tomb
which does not fly, your look which dares
   it to.

[C. W.]

ARGYLL TOUR
Glasgow

The kids under the cedar, fungi or mildew
fresh after wet weather,
the colt in a cage

con la scritta "mordace",
nafta a nubi, sospese
sui canali murati,
fumate di gabbiani, odor di sego
e di datteri, il mugghio del barcone,
catene che s'allentano
               – ma le tue le ignoravo –,
sulla scia
salti di tonni, sonno, lunghe strida
di sorci, oscene risa, anzi che tu
apparissi al tuo schiavo...

VERSO FINISTÈRE

Col bramire dei cervi nella piova
d'Armor l'arco del tuo ciglio s'è spento
al primo buio per filtrare poi
sull'intonaco albale dove prillano
ruote di cicli, fusi, razzi, frange
d'alberi scossi. Forse non ho altra prova
che Dio mi vede e che le tue pupille
d'acquamarina guardano per lui.

with the sign "beware,"
naphtha hung in clouds
over walled-in channels,
spirals of gulls, odor of suet
and piddocks, the lowing of barges,
chains easing off
           — but yours I was unaware of —,
in the wake
leaping tunny, sleep, squealings
of rats, obscene laughter, rather than you
appear to your slave. . .
                [C. C.]

TOWARDS FINISTÈRE

With the bellowing of the stags in the Armor
    rain,
the arc of your eyelash was quenched
in the first darkening to filter later
onto the dawn-washed plaster sky where
    bicycle wheels,
spindles, spokes and fringes of shaking trees
    whirl.
Perhaps I have no other proof that God sees
    me,
that your eyes, circles of aquamarine, still
    look for him.
             [C. W.]

SUL LLOBREGAT

Dal verde immarcescibile della canfora
due note, un intervallo di terza maggiore.
Il cucco, non la civetta, ti dissi; ma intanto, di scatt
tu avevi spinto l'acceleratore.

DAL TRENO

Le tortore colore solferino
sono a Sesto Calende per la prima
volta a memoria d'uomo. Cosí annunziano
i giornali. Affacciato al finestrino,
invano le ho cercate. Un tuo collare,
ma d'altra tinta, sí, piegava in vetta
un giunco e si sgranava. Per me solo
balenò, cadde in uno stagno. E il suo
volo di fuoco m'accecò sull'altro.

SIRIA

Dicevano gli antichi che la poesia
è scala a Dio. Forse non è cosí
se mi leggi. Ma il giorno io lo seppi

ON THE LLOBREGAT

From the incorruptible green of the camphor tree
two notes, an interval of a major third.
The cuckoo, not the screech-owl, I told you;
   but in the meantime,
         with a jerk,
you had jammed down the accelerator.

                      [C. W.]

FROM THE TRAIN

The bright-red turtle-doves
are at Sesto Calende for the first
time in living memory. So the papers
advertise. Face glued to the window,
in vain have I sought them. A collar of yours,
but of another hue, yes, a bulrush bowed
its head and was husked. For me only
did it flash, fall in a pool. And its
fiery flight blinded me to the other.

                      [C. C.]

SYRIA

Men of old have said that poetry
is the stairway to God. Perhaps it's not so
when you read me. But I knew it the day

che ritrovai per te la voce, sciolto
in un gregge di nuvoli e di capre
dirompenti da un greppo a brucar bave
di pruno e di falasco, e i volti scarni
della luna e del sole si fondevano,
il motore era guasto ed una freccia
di sangue su un macigno segnalava
la via di Aleppo.

INCANTESIMO

Oh resta chiusa e libera nell'isole
del tuo pensiero e del mio,
nella fiamma leggera che t'avvolge
e che non seppi prima
d'incontrare Diotima,
colei che tanto ti rassomigliava!
In lei vibra piú forte l'amorosa cicala
sul ciliegio del tuo giardino.
Intorno il mondo stringe; incandescente,
nella lava che porta in Galilea
il tuo amore profano, attendi l'ora
di scoprire quel velo che t'ha un giorno
fidanzata al tuo Dio.

you helped me recover my voice, loose
in a flock of clouds and goats
bursting out of a ditch to browse slaver
of blackthorn and marshgrass, and the
    unfleshed faces
of the moon and the sun melted together,
the car broke down and an arrow
of blood on a stone pointed
the way to Aleppo.

                    [C. C.]

SPELLBOUND

O stay closed and free in the islands
of your thought and mine,
in the buoyant flame which surrounds you
and which I did not know before
meeting Diotima,
she who so resembled you!
In her the amorous cicada vibrates louder
in the cherry tree of your garden.
Around, the world tightens; incandescent,
in the lava which brings to Galilee
your earthly love, you wait for the hour
to discover that veil which one day
betrothed you to your God.

                    [C. W.]

IRIDE

Quando di colpo San Martino smotta
le sue braci e le attizza in fondo al cupo
fornello dell'Ontario,
schiocchi di pigne verdi fra la cenere
o il fumo d'un infuso di papaveri
e il Volto insanguinato sul sudario
che mi divide da te;
                    questo e poco altro (se poco
è un tuo segno, un ammicco, nella lotta
che me sospinge in un ossario, spalle
al muro, dove zàffiri celesti
e palmizi e cicogne su una zampa non chiudono
l'atroce vista al povero
Nestoriano smarrito);

                    è quanto di te giunge dal naufragio
delle mie genti, delle tue, or che un fuoco
di gelo porta alla memoria il suolo
ch'è tuo e che non vedesti; e altro rosario
fra le dita non ho, non altra vampa
se non questa, di resina e di bacche,
t'ha investito.

★ ★ ★

Cuore d'altri non è simile al tuo,
la lince non somiglia al bel soriano
che apposta l'uccello mosca sull'alloro;
ma li credi tu eguali se t'avventuri

IRIS

When suddenly St. Martin's summer* topples
its embers and shakes them down low in
Ontario's dark hearth —
snapping of green pine cones in the cinders
or the fumes of steeped poppies
and the bloody Face on the shroud
that separates me from you:
                             this and little else (if very
little is in fact your sign, a nod, in the struggle
goading me into the charnel house, my back
to the wall, where the sapphires of heaven
and palm leaves and one-legged storks don't
    shut out
the brutal sight from the wretched
strayed Nestorian);
                     this is how much of you gets here
from the wreck of my people, and yours,
now that the fires of frost remind me of your
land which you've not seen; and I have
no other rosary to finger, no other flame
has assailed you, if it's not this,
of berries and resin.

The hearts of others are nothing like yours,
the lynx not like the striped tabby, beautiful,
alert for the hummingbird above the laurel;
but do you believe them the same breed,
    when you

*Indian summer

fuor dell'ombra del sicomoro
o è forse quella maschera sul drappo bianco,
quell'effigie di porpora che t'ha guidata?

Perché l'opera tua (che della Sua
è una forma) fiorisse in altre luci
Iri del Canaan ti dileguasti
in quel nimbo di vischi e pugnitopi
che il tuo cuore conduce
nella notte nel mondo, oltre il miraggio
dei fiori del deserto, tuoi germani.

Se appari, qui mi riporti, sotto la pergola
di viti spoglie, accanto all'imbarcadero
del nostro fiume – e il burchio non torna indietr
il sole di San Martino si stempera, nero.
Ma se ritorni non sei tu, è mutata
la tua storia terrena, non attendi
al traghetto la prua,
non hai sguardi, né ieri né domani;

perché l'opera Sua (*che nella tua*
si trasforma) *dev'esser continuata.*

venture outside the sycamore's shade
or maybe that mask on the white cloth
has guided you, that image in crimson?

So that your work (a form born of
His) might bloom under new suns
Iris of Canaan, you were gone
in that nimbus of mistletoe and thornbush
ushering your heart through the world's
nighttime, past the mirage
of desert flowers, your first kin.

If you turn up, here's where you'd bring me,
   the arbor
of stripped vines, next to our river's
pier — and the ferry does not come back
   again,
St. Martin's sun is blacked out.
But it won't be you, should you return, your
   earthly
story is changed, you don't wait for
the prow at the crossing,

       you have eyes for nothing, and no
         yesterdays or tomorrows;

       because His work (which translates
       into yours) *must be kept going.*

               [S. R. and A. de P.]

NELLA SERRA

S'empí d'uno zampettío
di talpe la limonaia,
brillò in un rosario di caute
gocce la falce fienaia.

S'accese sui pomi cotogni,
un punto, una cocciniglia,
si udí inalberarsi alla striglia
il poney – e poi vinse il sogno.

Rapito e leggero ero intriso
di te, la tua forma era il mio
respiro nascosto, il tuo viso
nel mio si fondeva, e l'oscuro

pensiero di Dio discendeva
sui pochi viventi, tra suoni
celesti e infantili tamburi
e globi sospesi di fulmini

su me, su te, sui limoni...

NEL PARCO

Nell'ombra della magnolia
che sempre piú si restringe,

IN THE GREENHOUSE

A pattering of moles
filled up the lemon trees,
in a rosary of cautious drops
the scythe was glittering.

Upon quinces ignited
a point, a lady-bug; the pony
was heard to rear under the curry-comb
— then dreaming overcame.

Ravished, all air, I was permeated
by you, your form became my own
hidden breathing, your
face melted into mine, and the obscure

idea of God descended
upon the few living, among
celestial soundings and infant drummings
and hanging spheres of lightnings,

upon me, and you, and the lemon trees. . .

[J. M.]

IN THE PARK

In the magnolia's ever
stricter shade, at one

131

a un soffio di cerbottana
la freccia mi sfiora e si perde.

Pareva una foglia caduta
dal pioppo che a un colpo di vento
si stinge – e fors'era una mano
scorrente da lungi tra il verde.

Un riso che non m'appartiene
trapassa da fronde canute
fino al mio petto, lo scuote
un trillo che punge le vene,

e rido con te sulla ruota
deforme dell'ombra, mi allungo
disfatto di me sulle ossute
radici che sporgono e pungo

con fili di paglia il tuo viso...

L'ORTO

Io non so, messaggera
che scendi, prediletta
del mio Dio (del tuo forse) se nel chiuso
dei meli lazzeruoli ove si lagnano
i luí nidaci, estenuanti a sera,

puff from a blowgun
the dart grazes me and is gone.

It was like a leaf let fall
by the poplar a gust of wind
uncolors − perhaps a hand
roving through green from afar.

A laughter not my own
pierces through hoary branches
into my breast, a thrill
shakes me, stabs my veins,

and I laugh with you on the warped
wheel of shade, I stretch out
discharged of myself on the sharp
protruding roots, and needle

your face with bits of straw. . .

[J. M.]

THE ORCHARD

I do not know, messenger
in descent, whom my god cherishes
(yours too, perhaps), if in the crab-tree grove
where the fledgling wrens mourn
languishing at nightfall,

io non so se nell'orto
dove le ghiande piovono e oltre il muro
si sfioccano, aerine, le ghirlande
dei carpini che accennano
lo spumoso confine dei marosi, una vela
tra corone di scogli
sommersi o nerocupi o piú lucenti
della prima stella che trapela –

io non so se il tuo piede
attutito, il cieco incubo onde cresco
alla morte dal giorno che ti vidi,
io non so se il tuo passo che fa pulsar le vene
se s'avvicina in questo intrico,
è quello che mi colse un'altra estate
prima che una folata
radente contro il picco irto del Mesco
infrangesse il mio specchio, –
io non so se la mano che mi sfiora la spalla
è la stessa che un tempo
sulla celesta rispondeva a gemiti
d'altri nidi, da un fólto ormai bruciato.

L'ora della tortura e dei lamenti
che s'abbatté sul mondo,

I do not know if in the orchard
where the acorns rain and where beyond the
  wall
the hornbeams shed their airy garlands and
  point out
the foamy border of the waves, a sail
between crowns of rock
submerged or darkblack or more gleaming
than the first start that breaks –

I do not know whether your muffled step,
blind nightmare whereby from the day I saw
  you
I have grown toward death,
I do not know whether your step
that makes my veins throb
to its approach here in this labyrinth
is the same step that overtook me in another
  summer
before a gale grazing the upthrust peak of
  Mesco
shattered my mirror. . .
I do not know whether the hand grazing my
  shoulder
is the same hand that once
at the celesta keyboard answered calls
from other nests and from a thicket long
  since burned.
The hour of torture and lament
that struck down on the world,

135

l'ora che tu leggevi chiara come in un libro
figgendo il duro sguardo di cristallo
bene in fondo, là dove acri tendíne
di fuliggine alzandosi su lampi
di officine celavano alla vista
l'opera di Vulcano,
il dí dell'Ira che piú volte il gallo
annunciò agli spergiuri,
non ti divise, anima indivisa,
dal supplizio inumano, non ti fuse
nella caldana, cuore d'ametista.

O labbri muti, aridi dal lungo
viaggio per il sentiero fatto d'aria
che vi sostenne, o membra che distinguo
a stento dalle mie, o diti che smorzano
la sete dei morenti e i vivi infocano,
o intento che hai creato fuor della tua misura
le sfere del quadrante e che ti espandi
in tempo d'uomo, in spazio d'uomo, in furie
di dèmoni incarnati, in fronti d'angiole
precipitate a volo... Se la forza
che guida il disco *di già inciso* fosse
un'altra, certo il tuo destino al mio
congiunto mostrerebbe un solco solo.

the hour you fore-read clear as though by book
fixing your hard crystal glance
full to the depths where acrid veils
of soot rising on flashes from the forge-room
barred from view
the handiwork of Vulcan,
the day of Wrath which more than once the
    cock
proclaimed unto the perjured,
did not divide you, undivided soul,
from the inhuman anguish, did not fuse you
within the cauldron, heart of amethyst.

O mute lips dry
from the long journey down the pathway
    made of air
that bore you, O limbs
I cannot tell apart from mine, O fingers slaking
the thirst of the dying and kindling those
    that live,
O purpose exceeding your own compass,
    having formed
the hands of the dial and expanding
into human time, into human space, in rages
of incarnate demons, in brows of angels
sped down in flight. . . If the force
that turns the disc *already cut*
were another, your destiny bound up with
    mine
would show a single groove.

                        [I. B.]

PRODA DI VERSILIA

I miei morti che prego perché preghino
per me, per i miei vivi com'io invece
per essi non resurrezione ma
il compiersi di quella vita ch'ebbero
inesplicata e inesplicabile, oggi
piú di rado discendono dagli orizzonti aperti
quando una mischia d'acque e cielo schiude
finestre ai raggi della sera, – sempre
piú raro, astore celestiale, un cutter
bianco-alato li posa sulla rena.

Broli di zinnie tinte ad artificio
(nonne dal duro sòggolo le annaffiano,
chiuse lo sguardo a chi di fuorivia
non cede alle impietose loro mani
il suo male), cortili di sterpaglie
incanutite dove se entra un gatto
color frate gli vietano i rifiuti
voci irose; macerie e piatte altane
su case basse lungo un ondulato
declinare di dune e ombrelle aperte
al sole grigio, sabbia che non nutre
gli alberi sacri alla mia infanzia, il pino
selvatico, il fico e l'eucalipto.

BEACH AT VERSILIA

I pray for my dead so that they might pray
for me; for my living because I ask for them
not resurrection but, instead, the fulfillment
of that life they have had
unexplained, and unexplainable; today
seldom one sees them descend from the open
   horizons
when riots of water and sky open
windows to the tentacles of the evening —
   more and more often
a cutter, the sky-hung goshawk, white-crested,
white-pinioned, lowers them to the sand.

Beds of zinnias dyed like wax flowers
(grandmothers with stiff, chin-strapped
  head-wear water them,
refusing to look at anyone from the outside
   street
who won't surrender his sickness
into their unpitying hands); courtyards of
   grizzled, whitened
brushwood where angry voices
refuse left-overs to the friar-colored cat
if he dare enter; rubble and flat over-looks
on low houses along an undulating
descent of dunes, and umbrellas opened
against a grey sun; sand that can't nourish
the trees sacred to my childhood, the wild pine,
the fig and the eucalyptus.

A quell'ombre i primi anni erano folti,
gravi di miele, pur se abbandonati;
a quel rezzo anche se disteso sotto
due brandelli di crespo punteggiati
di zanzare dormivo nella stanza
d'angolo, accanto alla cucina, ancora
nottetempo o nel cuore d'una siesta
di cicale, abbagliante nel mio sonno,
travedevo oltre il muro, al lavandino,
care ombre massaggiare le murene
per respingerne in coda, e poi reciderle,
le spine; a quel perenne alto stormire
altri perduti con rastrelli e forbici
lasciavano il vivaio
dei fusti nani per i sempreverdi
bruciati e le cavane avide d'acqua.

Anni di scogli e di orizzonti stretti
a custodire vite ancora umane
e gesti conoscibili, respiro
o anelito finale di sommersi
simili all'uomo o a lui vicini pure
nel nome: il pesce prete, il pesce rondine,
l'àstice – il lupo della nassa – che
dimentica le pinze quando Alice

Under those shadows my early years were
    crowded,
heavy with honey even now, so long
    abandoned;
in that shade, often spread out under
only two strips of crepe-paper riddled
with mosquitos, I slept — there, and in the
    corner room,
next to the kitchen, at nighttime;
in the deeps of siestas
while cicadas jangled, dazzling in my sleep,
I sometimes would catch a glimpse, over the
    wall, at the wash-basin,
of the shadows of loved ones massaging
    the moray eels,
forcing the bones back to the tails, then
    cutting them out;
in that endless high humming
others now gone, with rakes and shears
would leave the nursery
of dwarf stalks for the burnt
evergreens, for the channels greedy for water.

Those years of beech reefs and closed horizons
were custodians of lives still human,
of acts still understandable — like the breathing,
like the final sigh of underwater creatures
then similar to man: the priest fish,
    the swallow fish,
the lobster — wolf of the traps — who
forgot his pinchers when Alice

gli si avvicina... e il volo da trapezio
dei topi familiari da una palma
all'altra; tempo che fu misurabile
fino a che non s'aperse questo mare
infinito, di creta e di mondiglia.

LA PRIMAVERA HITLERIANA

Né quella ch'a veder lo sol si gira... (Dante (?) a Giovanni Quirini)

Folta la nuvola bianca delle falene impazzite
turbina intorno agli scialbi fanali e sulle spallette,
stende a terra una coltre su cui scricchia
come su zucchero il piede; l'estate imminente sprigiona
ora il gelo notturno che capiva
nelle cave segrete della stagione morta,
negli orti che da Maiano scavalcano a questi renai.

Da poco sul corso è passato a volo un messo infernale
tra un alalà di scherani, un golfo mistico acceso
e pavesato di croci a uncino l'ha preso e inghiottito,
si sono chiuse le vetrine, povere

came near. . . and the trapeze acts
of familiar mice from one palm tree
to the other — time that once was measurable
until this endless sea opened,
this sea of clay and dead droppings.

[C. W.]

THE HITLER SPRING

The dense white cloud of the mayflies crazily
Whirls around the pallid street lamps
      and over the parapets,
Spreads on the ground a blanket on
      which the foot
Grates as on sprinkled sugar; the looming
      summer now
Releases the nightfrosts which it was
      holding
In the secret caves of the dead season,
In the gardens of Maiano where the
      sandpits stop.

And soon over the street an infernal
      messenger passes in flight;
The murderers salute; a mystical gulf, fired
And beflagged with swastikas, has taken
      and swallowed us;
The shopwindows, humble and inoffensive,
      are closed

e inoffensive benché armate anch'esse
di cannoni e giocattoli di guerra,
ha sprangato il beccaio che infiorava
di bacche il muso dei capretti uccisi,
la sagra dei miti carnefici che ancora ignorano il sangue
s'è tramutata in un sozzo trescone d'ali schiantate,
di larve sulle golene, e l'acqua séguita a rodere
le sponde e piú nessuno è incolpevole.

Tutto per nulla, dunque? – e le candele
romane, a San Giovanni, che sbiancavano lente
l'orizzonte, ed i pegni e i lunghi addii
forti come un battesimo nella lugubre attesa
dell'orda (ma una gemma rigò l'aria stillando
sui ghiacci e le riviere dei tuoi lidi
gli angeli di Tobia, i sette, la semina
dell'avvenire) e gli eliotropi nati
dalle tue mani – tutto arso e succhiato
da un polline che stride come il fuoco
e ha punte di sinibbio...

Though armed – they also –
With cannon and toys of war;
The butcher has struck who dresses
    with flowers and berries
The muzzles of the slaughtered goats.
The ritual of the mild hangman,
    once innocent of blood,
Is changed to a spastic dance of
    shattering wings,
The mayflies' tiny deaths whiten the
    piers' edge
And the water continues to eat at the
Shoreline, and no one is any more blameless.

All for nothing, then? – and the Roman
    candles
At San Giovanni, which gradually
Blanched the horizon, and the pledges
    and the long farewells
Strong as a baptism, in the sorrowful
    expectation
Of the horde, (but a bud striped the air,
    distilling
On the ice and on the rivers of your country
The messengers of Tobias, the seven,
    the seeds
Of the future) and the heliotrope
Born of your hands – all burned, sucked
    dry
By a pollen that cries like fire
And is winged with ice and salt.

Oh la piagata
primavera è pur festa se raggela
in morte questa morte! Guarda ancora
in alto, Clizia, è la tua sorte, tu
che il non mutato amor mutata serbi,
fino a che il cieco sole che in te porti
si abbàcini nell'Altro e si distrugga
in Lui, per tutti. Forse le sirene, i rintocchi
che salutano i mostri nella sera
della loro tregenda, si confondono già
col suono che slegato dal cielo, scende, vince –
col respiro di un'alba che domani per tutti
si riaffacci, bianca ma senz'ali
di raccapriccio, ai greti arsi del sud...

O this ulcered
Spring will still be festival, if it can
    freeze again
In death that death! Observe once more
Up yonder, Clizia, your destiny, you
Preserved through change by a love
    which does not change
Until the blind sun you carry in you
Blinds itself in that other, and confounds
    itself
In Him, for all.

Perhaps the sirens and the bells
Which salute the monsters in the night
At their witch's sabbath are already
    confounded
With the sound which unloosed from
    heaven descends and conquers —
With the breath of a dawn which may
    yet reappear
Tomorrow, white but without wings
Of terror, to the parched arroyos of the south.

[M. E.]

Note on this poem. The season is Spring, the scene Florence,
the day that of the feast of San Giovanni, patron of the city,
whose festival is celebrated with fireworks. The moment is
that of the visit of the Fuehrer, who rides through the streets
accompanied by the Duce and their henchmen. The festival
thus becomes a grotesquely unholy holy day, whose real
meaning is symbolized by the forced closing of the shops; toy-
shops and butcher shops where, following custom, the young
goat is crowned with a garland as soon as it is killed.

VOCE GIUNTA CON LE FOLAGHE

Poiché la via percorsa, se mi volgo, è piú lunga
del sentiero da capre che mi porta
dove ci scioglieremo come cera,
ed i giunchi fioriti non leniscono il cuore
ma le vermene, il sangue dei cimiteri,
eccoti fuor dal buio
che ti teneva, padre, erto ai barbagli,
senza scialle e berretto, al sordo fremito
che annunciava nell'alba
chiatte di minatori dal gran carico
semisommerse, nere sull'onde alte.

L'ombra che mi accompagna
alla tua tomba, vigile,
e posa sopra un'erma ed ha uno scarto
altero della fronte che le schiara
gli occhi ardenti ed i duri sopraccigli
da un suo biocco infantile,
l'ombra non ha piú peso della tua
da tanto seppellita, i primi raggi
del giorno la trafiggono, farfalle
vivaci l'attraversano, la sfiora
la sensitiva e non si rattrappisce.

VOICE ARRIVING WITH THE COOTS

Since the road already travelled, if I
    turned back,
is longer than the goat path that takes me now
to where we shall melt like wax figurines,
and the bloomed weeds don't soothe the heart,
but only their own twigs and the
    blood of cemeteries,
here you are, father, outside
the dark that held you back, erect in the
    glare of the light,
without shawl or beret, in the dull shudder
which spoke out once in the dawn,
announcing the miners' barges half-underwater
from their great loads, black on the high waves.

The shadow that follows me, father,
to your grave, alert,
leans on a bust of Hermes, and has a proud
toss of the head that pushes back
from the forehead, from the burning eyes
    and thick eyebrows,
her childish wave of hair;
this shadow weighs no more than you do,
    father,
so long buried now — the first sun's rays
of the day transfix her, jerky
butterflies drift over her, a young plant
brushes against her, and does not scare.

L'ombra fidata e il muto che risorge,
quella che scorporò l'interno fuoco
e colui che lunghi anni d'oltretempo
(anni per me pesante) disincarnano,
si scambiano parole che interito
sul margine io non odo; l'una forse
ritroverà la forma in cui bruciava
amor di Chi la mosse e non di sé,
ma l'altro sbigottisce e teme che
la larva di memoria in cui si scalda
ai suoi figli si spenga al nuovo balzo.

– Ho pensato per te, ho ricordato
per tutti. Ora ritorni al cielo libero
che ti tramuta. Ancora questa rupe
ti tenta? Sí, la bàttima è la stessa
di sempre, il mare che ti univa ai miei
lidi da prima che io avessi l'ali,
non si dissolve. Io le rammento quelle
mie prode e pur son giunta con le folaghe
a distaccarti dalle tue. Memoria
non è peccato fin che giova. Dopo
è letargo di talpe, abiezione

che funghisce su sé... –

The faithful shadow and the new one
    rising up,
the one whom the inner fire disembodied
and the one whom long years in another place
(hard years for me) have stripped of flesh,
talk together, words which I, stock-still
on the edge of understanding, cannot hear.
    The one, perhaps,
will find again the order wherein love burned
for Him who moved her, and not for herself;
but the other is terrified and fears
that the warm ghost of a memory that he
    remains
to his sons will soon grow cold, and disappear.

"I have thought of you, I have remembered
for everyone. Now you return to the open sky
and everything changes. This cliff-line
still tempts you? Yes, the wave-reach
    is the same
as it always was, the sea that joins you
to my earlier beaches does not break up.
Calling to mind those shores, I
have arrived with the coots
to take you away from yours. Memory
isn't a sin so long as it does some good.
After that it's like the slow-wittedness
    of moles,
servility gone stale, and green with
    mould. . ."

Il vento del giorno
confonde l'ombra viva e l'altra ancora
riluttante in un mezzo che respinge
le mie mani, e il respiro mi si rompe
nel punto dilatato, nella fossa
che circonda lo scatto del ricordo.
Così si svela prima di legarsi
a immagini, a parole, oscuro senso
reminiscente, il vuoto inabitato
che occupammo e che attende fin ch'è tempo
di colmarsi di noi, di ritrovarci...

L'OMBRA DELLA MAGNOLIA

L'ombra della magnolia giapponese
si sfoltisce or che i bocci paonazzi
sono caduti. Vibra intermittente
in vetta una cicala. Non è più
il tempo dell'unísono vocale,
Clizia, il tempo del nume illimitato
che divora e rinsangua i suoi fedeli.
Spendersi era più facile, morire
al primo batter d'ale, al primo incontro
col nemico, un trastullo. Comincia ora

The wind of the day
mingles the live shadow and the other one
still holding back in a middle ground,
    a ground that thrusts away
my hands, and breaks my breath
in my full lungs, in the ditch
enclosing the start of memory.
Thus it slackens, before it can lock
onto the images, onto the words, onto the dark
remembering senses of the past, the emptiness
we once occupied which waits us again,
    when it is time
to take us back, to take us in.

[C. W.]

THE SHADOW OF THE MAGNOLIA

The shadow of the Japanese magnolia
thins out now that its purple buds
have fallen. At the top intermittently
a cigale vibrates. It is no longer
the time of the choir in unison, Sunflower,
the time of the unlimited godhead
whose faithful it devours that it may feed them.
It was easier to use oneself up, to die
at the first beating of wings, at the first
    encounter
with the enemy; that was child's play.
    Henceforth

la via piú dura: ma non te consunta
dal sole e radicata, e pure morbida
cesena che sorvoli alta le fredde
banchine del tuo fiume, – non te fragile –
fuggitiva cui zenit nadir cancro
capricorno rimasero indistinti
perché la guerra fosse in te e in chi adora
su te le stimme del tuo Sposo, flette
il brivido del gelo... Gli altri arretrano
e piegano. La lima che sottile
incide tacerà, la vuota scorza
di chi cantava sarà presto polvere
di vetro sotto i piedi, l'ombra è livida, -
è l'autunno, è l'inverno, è l'oltrecielo
che ti conduce e in cui mi getto, cèfalo
saltato in secco al novilunio.

                                    Addio.

L'ANGUILLA

L'anguilla, la sirena
dei mari freddi che lascia il Baltico
per giungere ai nostri mari,
ai nostri estuarî, ai fiumi
che risale in profondo, sotto la piena avversa,

begins the harder path: but not you, eaten
by sun, and rooted, and withal delicate
thrush soaring high above the cold
wharves of your river − not you, fragile
fugitive to whom zenith nadir cancer
capricorn remains indistinct
because the war was within you and within
whoso adores upon you the wounds of
   your Spouse,
flinch in the shivering frost. . . The others
retreat and shrivel. The file that subtly
engraves will be silenced, the empty husk
of the singer will soon be powdered
glass underfoot, the shade is livid −
it is autumn, it is winter, it is the beyond
that draws you and into which I throw
   myself, a mullet's
leap into dryness under the new moon.
Goodbye.
[J. M.]

THE EEL

The eel, the North Sea siren,
who leaves dead-pan Icelandic gods
and the Baltic for our Mediterranean,
our estuaries, our rivers −
who lances through their profound places,

di ramo in ramo e poi
di capello in capello, assottigliati,
sempre piú addentro, sempre piú nel cuore
del macigno, filtrando
tra gorielli di melma finché un giorno
una luce scoccata dai castagni
ne accende il guizzo in pozze d'acquamorta,
nei fossi che declinano
dai balzi d'Appennino alla Romagna;
l'anguilla, torcia, frusta,
freccia d'Amore in terra
che solo i nostri botri o i disseccati
ruscelli pirenaici riconducono
a paradisi di fecondazione;
l'anima verde che cerca
vita là dove solo
morde l'arsura e la desolazione,
la scintilla che dice
tutto comincia quando tutto pare
incarbonirsi, bronco seppellito;
l'iride breve, gemella
di quella che incastonano i tuoi cigli
e fai brillare intatta in mezzo ai figli
dell'uomo, immersi nel tuo fango, puoi tu
non crederla sorella?

and flinty portages, from branch to branch,
twig to twig, thinning down now,
ever snaking inward, worming
for the granite's heartland, threading
delicate capillaries of slime —
and in the Romagna one morning
the blaze of the chestnut blossoms
ignites its smudge in the dead water
pooled from chiselings
of the Apennines. . .
the eel, a whipstock, a Roman candle,
love's arrow on earth, which only
reaches the paradise of fecundity
through our gullies and fiery, charred streams;
a green spirit, potent only
where desolation and arson burn;
a spark that says everything
begins where everything is clinker;
this buried rainbow, this iris, twin sister
of the one you set in your eye's target center
to shine on the sons of men,
on us, up to our gills in your life-giving mud —
can you call her *Sister?*

                              [R. L.]

THE EEL

The eel, the
siren of sleety seas, abandoning
the Baltic for our waters,

our estuaries, our
freshets, to lash upcurrent under the brunt
of the flood, sunk deep, from brook to brook
   and then
trickle to trickle dwindling,
more inner always, always more in the heart
of the rock, thrusting
through ruts of the mud, until, one day,
explosion of splendor from the chestnut groves
kindles a flicker in deadwater sumps,
in ditches pitched
from ramparts of the Appennine to Romagna;
eel: torch and whip,
arrow of love on earth,
which nothing but our gorges or bone-dry
gutters of the Pyrenees usher back
to edens of fertility;
green soul that probes
for life where only
fevering heat or devastation preys,
spark that says
the whole commences when the whole
   would seem
charred black, an old stick buried;
brief rainbow, twin
to that within your lashes' dazzle, that
you keep alive, inviolate, among
the sons of men, steeped in your mire — in this
not recognize a sister?

              [J. F. N.]

PICCOLO TESTAMENTO

Questo che a notte balugina
nella calotta del mio pensiero,
traccia madreperlacea di lumaca
o smeriglio di vetro calpestato,
non è lume di chiesa o d'officina
che alimenti
chierico rosso, o nero.
Solo quest'iride posso
lasciarti a testimonianza
d'una fede che fu combattuta,
d'una speranza che bruciò piú lenta
di un duro ceppo nel focolare.
Conservane la cipria nello specchietto
quando spenta ogni lampada
la sardana si farà infernale
e un ombroso Lucifero scenderà su una prora
del Tamigi, del Hudson, della Senna
scuotendo l'ali di bitume semi-
mozze dalla fatica, a dirti: è l'ora.
Non è un'eredità, un portafortuna
che può reggere all'urto dei monsoni
sul fil di ragno della memoria,
ma una storia non dura che nella cenere
e persistenza è solo l'estinzione.
Giusto era il segno: chi l'ha ravvisato
non può fallire nel ritrovarti.
Ognuno riconosce i suoi: l'orgoglio
non era fuga, l'umiltà non era
vile, il tenue bagliore strofinato
laggiú non era quello di un fiammifero.

LITTLE TESTAMENT

This that at night keeps flashing
in the calotte of my mind,
mother-of-pearl trace of the snail
or emery of brayed glass,
is neither light of church or factory
that may sustain
clerical red, or black.
Only this iris can I
leave you as testimony
of a faith that was much disputed,
of a hope that burned more slowly
than a hard log in the fireplace.
Conserve its powder in your compact
when every lamplight spent
the sardana becomes infernal
and a shadowy Lucifer descends on a prow
of the Thames or Hudson or Seine
thrashing bituminous wings half-
shorn from the effort, to tell you: it's time.
There's no inheritance, no goodluck charm
that can ward off the monsoons' impact
on the gossamer of memory,
but a history endures in ashes alone
and persistence is only extinction.
Just was the sign: he who has realized it
cannot fail to find you again.
Everyone recognizes his own: pride
was not flight, humility was not
vile, the tenuous glitter polished up
down there was not that of a match.

[C. C.]

New Directions Paperbooks—A Partial Listing

For complete listing request free catalog from
New Directions, 80 Eighth Avenue, New York 10011

†Bilingual

For complete listing request free catalog from
New Directions, 80 Eighth Avenue, New York 10011   †Bilingual